SAVE YOURSELF MAMA

SAVE YOURSELF MAMA

A MUST-HAVE GUIDE TO UNDERSTANDING
YOUR RISK OF MATERNAL MORTALITY

IVY COCUZZI

THE SORREL LIFE PUBLISHING

I dedicate this book to my mom, Juliet, to Liz, my dearest friend, and to all the incredible women and mothers gone too soon on or after their journey to motherhood.

CONTENTS

Foreword

by Dr. Michael Hold

I am an obstetrician/gynecologist and I have a practice in Houston, Texas with many pregnant patients. When a mother gets pregnant and is about to have a baby, there is so much hope, joy, and anticipation. The birth of a child is supposed to be a very loud and happy experience, with the baby crying and the mother and father crying with joy. There are also loud cheers and praises from the staff and family in the delivery room.

However, sometimes things don't go as planned and something terrible and unexpected happens. Sometimes a baby is born, and it doesn't cry. In desperation, the mother and father ask what has happened to their baby while the neonatal team works to resuscitate the baby. Occasionally, a baby is found lifeless on an ultrasound when the mother comes to the hospital for a pregnancy related disease—then the baby is stillborn. Whenever I deliver these babies, no sound comes from the baby —this absence of sound pierces my ears like a knife.

The loudest sound in the world to me is the absence of sound.

My sister, Liz, was supposed to have delivered her little bundle of joy, Evan, but she died at home from an eclamptic seizure while sleeping. She never had the chance to see her baby or hear him cry. The only sound that was heard was the sound of Liz's husband screaming and crying when he found her in her bed cold, unresponsive, and silent. The ambulance came and the emergency team found that she was dead on arrival.

Liz had signs and symptoms, but she didn't recognize how serious her symptoms were.

She didn't realize the need to ask for help.

I pray this never happens to anyone ever again.

Every pregnant woman and new mother should understand that she puts her life on the line when she gets pregnant. Even though pregnancy is a natural state, it can cause very serious and life-threatening conditions every mother should know.

This book explores these conditions and gives patients the tools to advocate for themselves in a complex and confusing medical system. I hope that this book will save at least one life.

~Dr. Michael Hold

A Letter for Liz

Dear Liz,

I miss you tremendously my amazing little sister, and I think about you all the time. Your good friend, Ivy, has written a book about life-threatening conditions related to pregnancy so that mothers-to-be and new mothers can recognize the serious signs and symptoms of these diseases. She wrote this book so that they can advocate for themselves to avoid dying like you did. At the time of your death, I was doing a procedure in my OB-GYN office when your husband, Louis, called to tell me you and your unborn baby, Evan, had died. He said that you had a terrible headache, and

that you went to bed to take a nap, but you never
woke up. The shock of this hit me like a
sledgehammer. I could not believe it, but it was so
painfully true. My mind raced back through my life
with you. I remembered all the fun times and
adventures that you and I had growing up together.
I recalled all the parties, festivals, religious
celebrations, and overseas journeys we had together.
I always appreciated you listening to me and giving
me advice. I always valued your opinion, and I
considered you to be wise beyond your years. I am
sorry that I was not more involved with your
prenatal care, but I wanted to give you space to
make your own decisions about your pregnancy, but
this was an enormous mistake. I wish that I had
spoken more with you and Louis about the many
dangerous diseases associated with pregnancy, such
as eclampsia, which took your life and Evan's life.
As an obstetrician, I see and treat pre-eclampsia
before they have an eclamptic seizure, and those that
did present to the hospital with ecliptic seizures were
successfully treated and had full recoveries. I had
only read about patients who died from this
condition, and their deaths were in very distant
countries with limited medical care. How could this
have happened to you? You lived in Houston, Texas,
which has the largest medical center in the world. I
was an OB-GYN physician. How could this have

possibly happened to you? I am so sorry that I let you down, and I will forever have this sense of guilt for not speaking to you more frequently and more forcefully about what to look out for. After you died, I spoke to your doctor, and your doctor is extremely sorry for what happened to you. They honor your memory and pray for you every year on a pilgrimage. Your doctor did not mean for this to happen to you, and I know that they are truly very sorry. After a long struggle within me, I was able to forgive them for not identifying this disease and for not getting you hospitalized. I had to forgive them, because what happened to you could have happened to any of my pregnant patients. You were 36 weeks pregnant, and you would have survived if your baby, Evan, was delivered because that would have started the cure for pre-eclampsia. You were so close. You and your husband, Louis, were so happy when you were pregnant. You were glowing with joy and anticipation of meeting your baby, Evan, and I knew that you were going to be a wonderful mother. You always poured your heart into everything that you did. After you died, I initially had a hard time delivering babies, but I realized that I wanted to continue being an obstetrician. I felt that if I could save at least one mother's life, that it would help me cope with losing yours. So, I became involved with the hospital to help improve the safety of new mothers and mothers-to-be. I wanted you to know that there are some very important and positive changes happening in hospitals and doctor's offices across the country that will bring awareness to maternal diseases. These changes will provide improved treatments to help prevent maternal deaths like yours. I wanted to tell your story in front of my peers, but I am still coping with your loss. However, your good friend Ivy spoke to me as she wrote this manuscript, which is about the severe pregnancy related diseases every mother should know about. I was honored when she asked me to write this Foreword, which has brought me closer to you and closer to God. I am yearning to be closer to God.

Love always and forever,

Michael

Author's Note

Listen. Trust yourself. Speak up.

This is the theme of *Save Yourself Mama*.

Always listen to your gut if something doesn't feel right during and after your pregnancy. Speak up! Never give up if you are not heard or seen. If it means finding someone who will see you and listen to you, it is your right to demand that.

Our bodies are beautiful machines that give us warning signs when something is not well. Unfortunately, we are not always used to listening to our bodies. But during pregnancy, as mothers, we develop intuition about ourselves, our loved ones, and our children. You should never ignore those intuitive feelings. Whenever you are concerned, that is a good reason to seek care or attention.

Do not allow yourself or anyone else to minimize those feelings or tell you that something isn't wrong.

You are the captain of the beautiful ship that is your body.

You get to decide.

I'll share my story with you. When I gave birth to my twin daughters, they required care in the NICU. At the time, I focused only on my babies. I ignored the pain and warning signs that my body sent me. When I finally listened, I had to visit the emergency room. That trip opened my eyes to flaws in our healthcare system and society that, as a clinician, I had never seen.

The experience helped me connect the dots.

Suddenly, I saw connections to the poor systems and outcomes I had witnessed as a clinical student. I connected as a grand daughter who never met her maternal grandmother because she died during childbirth. I also connected as a daughter whose mother never got to live with her babies. I connected as a friend who had to bury her beautiful friend and baby in the last weeks of pregnancy. Lastly, I finally connected as someone who has heard countless stories of moms who feel blessed to still be here.

I knew it was important to share these stories. I hope to emphasize to all mothers: listen and be in tune with your normal physical state so you can notice when something is wrong.

Never be afraid of looking stupid.

Don't worry about wasting someone's time.

Don't dismiss your thoughts as "crazy."

Why? Because your life could be at stake! No one can come close to filling the role you play in your child's life. You must remain alive to nurture your children. You are worth it!

About "Save Yourself Mama"

Save Yourself Mama is a guide to help you understand your risk of having problems during or after pregnancy, and what it means to be a statistic of maternal mortality.

This guide will:

- Present prompts to help you to start the right conversations with your provider and health care team. To take a more active role in your own care, you must have knowledge.

- Show you the importance of cultivating a strong relationship with your birthing team.
- List the mental and physical warning signs of maternal distress and teach you how to get help immediately.
- Teach you to speak loudly when something feels wrong, while not allowing anyone to stifle your need to be seen and understood.
- Give helpful reminders of the roles that family, friends, and community members play to ensure you thrive and not only survive pregnancy during the first years after baby is born— when risks for physical or mental harm are highest.

Save Yourself Mama is divided into three parts:

- *Part I* includes stories and information to help you better understand and connect to the maternal issues that exist.
- *Part II* contains powerful actionable steps and content that will enable you to be empowered to understand and to better navigate the healthcare system.
- *Part III* highlights the benefits of sharing and writing out experiences and stories as well as note taking areas for reflection.

REGARDING THE TERM "MAMA"

Universally, "Mama" is what all babies call their mother. I understand that not everyone identifies as a woman or with the female gender. We respect and have provided this information to include all birthing persons regardless of their race, gender, or sexual orientation.

INTRODUCTION

All you need to look at is a country's maternal mortality rate. That is a surrogate for whether the country's health system is functioning.
—Margaret Chan

HOW IT STARTED

I REMEMBER the first day of my clinical rotations as a physician associate (PA). It was filled with so many emotions: triumph, happiness, and even tears. My career journey had been a hard road to travel. And that road included mountains of debt and the need to prove, to myself and my family, that I'd made the right decision. Even though, as I reflect, I don't know what that meant.

As an African immigrant, I understand now from a much-grounded perspective: my family feared my decision to 'only' complete a master level training in medicine and become a PA.

My confused parents would ask, "What will we tell people you have become? An assistant?"

Though I knew becoming a doctor was within reach for me, I also knew becoming a PA was a better fit for several reasons. The greater connection and bond formed with patients. The path for varied experiences and learning. The smaller amount of student debt. The shorter path to joining the workforce. Being independent. The physician's associate career path was limitless —I could choose any specialty I wanted, and literally experience as much of the healthcare world as I desired. The flexibility fascinated me more than my pride, so I chose to have a less than glamorous title that didn't convey the breadth of my competence or my desire to not become an MD.

MY FIRST DAY

My first day of rotations after surviving the brutal didactic part — three years of medical school crammed in one year — was the start of a six-week obstetrics and gynecology rotation. It was a blur — the hardest thing I had ever done in my professional journey. We actually lost a few students because of the rigorous nature of the courses and were warned of the toll the training had taken on the mental health of some students. But taking part in clinical rotations meant I had completed a major hurdle. I only needed to complete rotations and pass my boards to become a PA.

I reported to my location on the maternity ward and noticed we were all new to the rotation. There were also interns, medical students, and residents. We met with our team lead and another medical resident that day. Nervousness filled me as we assembled. I was the lowest on the totem pole. I thought perhaps I shouldn't be there since I wasn't in medical school. My schooling had provided lots of clinical information but hadn't prepared me with the innate confidence that I needed to be there.

We broke off into two smaller teams. My first two weeks of rotations was exhilarating. I assisted the clinical and midwifery teams with delivering several babies. Our patient population was new to me. It was very diverse, with Hispanic and black mothers as young as sixteen. Many didn't speak English and required translation help. I couldn't put myself in their place. Even the 25-year-old mothers seemed so young. I was twenty-three at the time and hadn't yet had a long-term boyfriend. As an immigrant I was only cleared to date when I finished school, and I had been in school a while. The thought of having a child of my own seemed unfathomable. I could only relate to the women as patients requiring care.

As I write this, I am now a mother. I wonder what my experience would have been had I been able to hold hands with those women and truly understand the pregnancy journey of young women of color.

What dots would I have connected for them?

Could I have been an advocate for change?

Would I have intervened much earlier?

MY RESIDENT EXPERIENCE

As I progressed in my OB-GYN rotation, I was fascinated with this field of bringing babies into the world. I saw severe complications, routine care, and advanced procedures.

I thought, *yes, I have found my niche!*

This was what I wanted to study! How did anyone not think it was the coolest specialty there?

I thought this after only ONE WEEK.

One night I was paired with an OB-GYN resident, and I was less nervous than my first day. I was comfortable getting history and physicals and assessments. The residents I followed were appreciative — this helped reduce their workload, which was immense. Personally, I was glad to help and not be a hindrance and heavy luggage they had to tow around during their shift. But that night, my resident was tired. He frowned constantly. It was his third shift in a row, and it showed! He was short-tempered, gave me the silent treatment, and only wanted 'need-to-know' information from everyone around me. I held my breath and tried not to get in his way — I wanted to stay on Grumpy's good side.

We started working up obstetric cases in the EC from women

who had complaints. My resident and I got separated as I wrapped up my assessment in one room. The plan was to meet up and debrief. I was waiting for him outside the room, and by room it was an area designated by curtains, I jumped up as he walked out, swiping the curtain out of his way aggressively that gave me a glimpse into the room and the patient he had been seeing. She was in her twenties—a young Hispanic female. Her husband was by her side. With her hand on her belly, she wore a worried look on her face. Her English was understandable, but I had to strain to hear her words.

The resident rushed past me, his face grim. Determined, I chased him and asked what was wrong with the patient.

"She is here again. I saw her yesterday! There is nothing wrong with her and she needs to go home!" he grumbled.

I glanced back. I knew he hadn't been in there long enough to have assessed her, at least not fully.

I'm not sure why, but I offered to help. "Why don't I do her H&P and work her up fully? I can let you know once I'm done," I said.

He waved his hand as if to say, *be my guest if that's how you want to waste your time.*

Working with her gave him a break from keeping me as a shadow. It was an extremely busy night. The workload seemed endless. How would we get to all these patients?

I returned to the room and scanned the worry on her face.

"Don't worry. We will examine you." I assured her.

I asked her our typical questions, and she provided answers. It turned out this was not her first pregnancy, and she was expecting twins. She was about 23 weeks along.

I was excited. I'd never seen a case of multiples up close before.

But the patient kept saying she experienced bleeding and, as I interpreted from her broken English, all didn't feel right "there."

She was a thin woman, so I lay her back and quickly prepared to do a vaginal exam. The second I removed her underwear, I saw it: a tiny hand coming out of the vaginal opening.

I must have screamed and called out. The nurses heard me and rushed in. When they saw what I'd glimpsed, their horrified faces reflected my own.

I blurted to the patient. "We need to get you to the operating room quickly! I can see your baby!"

She started crying, and I held her hand. The resident rushed in, and I relayed all the information I knew. The hospital staff were prepping the operating room, and we were going with her. He debriefed the attending over the phone and in what seemed like five minutes we were already in the operating theater. We scrubbed in and I observed. The patient had an emergency C-section with the Neonatal Intensive Care Unit (NICU) team standing by.

The first baby entered the world looking bruised and lanky—his limbs swung about as the delivery team put him down and began CPR.

The second baby arrived onto a second warmer, and once again, CPR started immediately.

I'd never seen so many people fit into one operating room.

After a short time, 'baby A' team backed away slowly, shaking their heads. Then 'baby B' team, heads down, also moved away. The surgeons were delivering the placenta and closing up the patient. All their actions became a confusing blur to me. When the medical staff wheeled the babies out, my feet felt frozen to the floor. I stayed with the mother. I couldn't bring myself to leave her alone. Once she was closed up, she was transferred to a wheelchair. Nurses wheeled her to the adjacent area—a round room with incubators in the corner. It was a recovery room, but she was the only patient surrounded by what seemed like over thirty medical providers. She remained silent, as she didn't speak English. Her circulating nurse rubbed her shoulders. She asked for her babies repeatedly. Nurses brought them to her, lifeless to hold while they told her the twins did not survive.

The patient gave a gut-wrenching howl. I can still hear to this day. "No no no no no. Nooooooooooooooooo!"

I glanced about the room, catching the eyes of anyone to please tell her we got it wrong. That, in fact, the babies were fine. Everyone remained still. Tears appeared on the nurse's faces. All eyes fixated on the mother. It didn't seem right that we were all there… watching her. I wished for her to be in her own room. I wasn't sure how I walked to the room—it was like I was still in a daze. Shock filled me and I wondered how this had happened.

The mother held her babies and stared at them. She got quiet and held them to her lips, as if to nuzzle them, speaking to them in her native language as tears streamed down her face. I don't remember how long she held her twins, but to me, as a mother today, it seemed not long enough.

I don't know how I transitioned from that moment to the next in order to attend to another patient who needed our attention. For me and the rest of the medical team, the babies' deaths were a sad stamp in our day. For the patient, I shudder to consider how she felt. I would love to have known or checked in on her in a day, a week, a month. I wished I could do anything to change her outcome.

We returned to our jobs, and in our heads I'm sure we all filed the experience under a very sad, unfortunate event. Just one of those things that happen. We win some. We lose some. Multiple providers talked about the "circle of life".

I've mentally replayed the case repeatedly throughout my career. To this day the questions haunt me.

Did we really do our best for that patient?

Could we all just say… that's life?

How long had the mother been trying to get someone's attention?

Were those babies' deaths preventable?

Why had medical staff sent her home before?

If someone had stepped in sooner, would the mother's babies have survived?

Did the medical team truly review each case with scrutiny regarding poor outcomes?

Did they look at the visit frequencies and consider patterns?

Did we all miss opportunities to save those babies?

MY "WHY"

I wish I could say I asked those questions that day. I didn't. It has taken over 15 years for me to bravely ask those questions. The horrifying moments became the driving force in my career — the reason I will never be satisfied with being "just an immigrant". I'm a mom, I'm a black woman, I'm an advanced practice provider (APP) who practiced neurosurgery, emergency medicine, oncology, and ultrasound guided procedures. I became a frontline leader in an institution that inspired me to take a hard look at the stories I personally took part in. Many of the stories troubled me and made me ask *why?*

Why does this happen to women?

Why wasn't anything changing quickly?

It led me to seek more knowledge especially after undergoing my own experience as a woman of color when I gave birth to my babies. I thought my education would protect me, my socioeconomic status also. No, the statistics were true… this was a true disparity for African American women, the usual social determinants or factors that would be protective for other races were not for me. So, I returned to school to study public health and social work. I needed to find answers to these big questions.

Why do some people receive better care than others?

Why do preventable deaths happen?

As I write this book, I look forward to my forties because of the escalating wisdom those years will bring. Aging becomes a new superpower. Though our smooth skin may trade places with wrinkles, or our hair may turn gray, the pieces of the puzzle come together based on our experience. We connect the dots more easily. After years of giving to others, our parents, families, jobs, aging provides the opportunity to give to ourselves through our passions. We can inadvertently help our communities through answering our inner calling to serve.

During my clinical training days, I wanted to hide some of my identities—the ones that made me feel as though I shouldn't be here. My accent. My status as an unmarried, black, female, immigrant. And later, my status as a divorced black female immigrant. Today, my training and life experiences have shown it is my own unique combination of identities and experiences that make me uniquely me.

There is no other me, just like there is no other you.

Your power is in owning and proudly and unapologetically wearing every identity and experience that makes you who you are: your race, culture, gender, sexual orientation, religion, education level, and socioeconomic status. It is in that beautiful combination that we embrace our passion and purpose proudly to do what we love or learn more about and use it to serve others. Your identity combination allows you to have a unique voice from which to tell your extraordinary version of how you see the world.

After reading this guide, I hope you tell your story so that we can change the world for the mamas who will come after us.

For our babies.

PART ONE

THE PERILS OF PREGNANCY

The Big Picture of Pregnancy

"It is the most powerful creation to have life growing inside of you. There is no bigger gift."

—*Beyoncé*

BEAUTIFUL MAMA, when you first heard those words "you are having a baby," those next feelings of immense unexplainable joy, then wonder, then the tears, especially for those whose journey to hear those words were filled with obstacles and pain.

The feelings that followed were probably fear and anxiety.

Then, *ok now what*?

How do you learn to support, and nurture your baby safely? Are you ready? Where do you get the information? Some of you were given stacks of books, online apps with developmental calendars for baby, and explanations of what you should eat or avoid eating. And let's not forget the gear you will need— enough to fill a small house, especially if having multiples.

You may have been surrounded by people who effortlessly brought their babies into the world with no issues and no complications. You saw the beautiful pictures of babies being held either at the hospital or at home if a home birth. There was no mention of the labor process, or the hours spent screaming or the healing after a C-section. No indication of the silence of the ones who didn't make it through. No discussion about the mothers and babies who experienced devastating complications.

Few books dedicate themselves to discussing what can and does wrong during pregnancy.

Fewer books talk about what you can do to prevent pregnancy complications.

If you've watched the news recently, more is being said about America's ranking for maternal mortality. This risk is higher for African American mothers, who are 3 to 5 times more likely to lose their lives on their journey to motherhood.

As an African mother, I wasn't aware of these risks during my pregnancy. I was mostly afraid of COVID, and honestly, I only cared that my babies survived. In my experience as a clinician and a friend, I had seen mothers lose their lives. I had lost a dear friend to pre-eclampsia, but system wide, I never thought the color of my skin would play a role in my pregnancy outcome or how I would be treated.

However, something happened to me. And it surprised me. Together with all the events I had witnessed surrounding maternal morbidity and mortality, you can say it was the straw that broke the camel's back.

If this happened to me, how did others stand a chance in our system?

I have unique experiences and education that have enabled me to connect the dots and realize that I can do my part to join the ongoing efforts to protect mothers to enable them to know their worth and the important role they play and can play in navigating the health care systems.

After reading this book, I can promise you will know your role. You will understand how much power you have, and how you can protect that power.

You CAN take steps to gain more control.

KNOWING YOUR PREGNANT BODY

Years ago, I never realized the miracle that is pregnancy. Even my doctors didn't realize it. Pregnancy is a feat that the body performs every day for millions of women. It is a huge miracle. I realized my ignorance stemmed not from my lack of knowledge per se, because I had read the medical books. I had some clinical training. I had delivered 15 babies in a hospital and emergency setting and once in a hot parking lot in Texas. I understood a few things, or so I thought. But in all my experience I never stopped to appreciate the entire gravity that is pregnancy how the human body supports life for nine months, more or less, 24/7. Pregnancy doesn't compare to any other physical stress. We also don't understand exactly how it affects every organ in our body, or exactly how our bodies change to create and support life.

The reasons are obvious now, as I continue to study maternal health, why in some ways we have made incredible advances, but in others not so much. For one reason, it is hard to study pregnant women and balance ethics and safety. Also, people don't think there is much else to know or figure out. We deliver healthy babies every day. This gives the medical community a false sense that they've "got it." But my personal experiences showed me we don't, especially when some providers I interacted with would tell me, "I don't know why this is happening to you. I don't know what is happening to you." An inner turmoil can brew inside you when your providers don't have a diagnosis of what is going on with you. When they shrug and look nervous. Honestly, it's scary.

No, you don't have to have attended medical school to gain a deeper understanding of what your body goes through so that you can be aware. And yes, there are the common changes we know about. That is not my focus, but I want you to see your body as a system. The changes of pregnancy are not independent of each other but all work together to support this life, it is from this basis that I want you to know that not all of us have the young fertile healthy bodies that can go through these monumental changes so you should think about how your body may be worked harder, stressed more, or sometimes have a hard go at it, and have these earnest conversations with your provider so that you can be prepared and recognize when something goes wrong.

Your pregnancy health does not just deal with your body and what or whether you can handle it physically. Stress, your environment, support systems, and your mental well-being must be considered. This is not an anatomical detailed review of how pregnancy affects the body, but a highlight of the effects on a few key organs in pregnancy that surprised me and that you should know so that you can be more informed and discuss with your health team if any issues arise for you or exist in your history.

BRAIN AND MENTAL HEALTH

Research has shown that for at least the first two years after pregnancy, our brains go through a change similar to that of when we all went through puberty. So, think hormones. There is an abundance of estrogen and progesterone during pregnancy, and this is speculated to make the brain more efficient in certain areas by shrinking the gray matter which helps it be more mature and efficient and do what it needs to do which is focus on baby and recognize when baby needs something, also so that you can attach to baby. This shrinkage could lead to the memory loss we fondly call *mommy brain*. The body prepares you to focus on supporting life. According to research, your ability to tend to other people socially, exhibit sensitivity to the emotion of others, and have intuition (recognize what is going on with others) are most affected.

In a nutshell, your brain changes so that you can protect your babies from harm and also bond with and love them.

So where does this go wrong?

Why do some women grow depressed, overly anxious, or

hallucinate, or have thoughts of harming themselves or their infants even after the delivery? This is the part we don't yet fully understand. We are still studying. Physically and mentally, we don't all start at the same point in pregnancy. There are so many factors to consider. Genetics. Past trauma. Mental health history. Former addictions. Low sleep. No sleep. Stress. In addition, the sudden hormone drop that affects the balance of neurotransmitters like serotonin and dopamine after pregnancy affects us all differently. You can think of it like an addict withdrawing from drugs. The severe dip can increase anxiety, cause depression, psychosis, and kick start mental disorders. Especially when there is familial history. So much is unknown. But knowing that your brain may respond differently than others to all the pregnancy changes is important. Also, without intervention research shows that symptoms can worsen with subsequent pregnancies. It is also important that your family and providers know so that your support systems can advocate for you.

Please don't be afraid that you are weird or different if you develop mental health issues after or during pregnancy. It is only your body responding to the rapid hormone changes. We all respond so differently, so have an honest conversation especially if you have already had mental health issues, substance abuse history or have issues in your family history so that you and your providers can expect and maybe consider starting or continuing medications or getting therapy in place early, even during pregnancy. Also, keeping family support at all-time high levels to minimize stress and get the very important sleep your brain needs. Research shows support is an amazing buffer for this. The stigma on mental health is real. This is different in various cultures, so please think outside of the box here if you have to. The effect of not recognizing and addressing these mental health issues early can, at worst, increase the risk of suicide, infanticide, cause decreased bonding with your infant, which research shows, can affect the relationship between mother and baby and the physical and mental health and development of the infant. Any of us can have this happen so be vigilant.

IMMUNE SYSTEM

The immune system has been a bit of a mystery. Researchers are still studying exactly how pregnancy affects it. Initial research showed that, because the body wants to protect your baby, and not have the immune system attack it, that the immune system grew weaker. Recent research now shows it is more complex than that. The fighter immune cells in your body actually increase in predictable timed phases. The reason you may grow sicker or feel worse while having the flu is because you have a stronger response to any bacteria or virus you get. The way your immune response behaves in pregnancy may even tell scientists in the future if you may deliver your baby early or not. So, what should you be aware of for your status? Do you have a known weakened immune system going into pregnancy? Do you have an autoimmune disease such as multiple sclerosis or lupus?

I'll give you an example. A year before my pregnancy I developed Graves' disease. Graves' disease affects the thyroid. My doctor and I discussed the disease even though I removed my thyroid before I got pregnant.

What can you do to optimize your immune system, knowing the key role it plays in supporting a healthy pregnancy? Optimize your immune system. Get as much sleep as possible. Drink lots of water and get regular exercise. Reduce your stress levels through meditation or yoga. Make sure vitamins, greens, and fruit, and all the macro nutrients of a balanced diet are a part of your daily living. All of these things help your immune system respond well. Also, make sure you are up to date on all your immunizations. Let your doctor know if you are struggling in these areas so you can come up together with practical solutions. Remember, when you are sick, baby gets sick too, so do your part!

HEART

The heart is an organ we grossly underestimate regarding the effects of pregnancy. The heart becomes such a powerful machine during this time. It rapidly takes on the work of almost 40% more blood volume to sustain both mom and baby. According to researchers, the heart increases both mass and the surrounding vessels to support mother and baby. The level of heart changes is much higher than, let's say, an athlete who has been training for years. Mom's body is literally working out 24/7 for nine months. No breaks. The heart works hand in hand with the placenta to move food to the baby.

What does this mean for you, dear mama? It means you should really think about your history if you have heart conditions while pregnant. Are you on blood pressure medication? Do you have an arrhythmia? Pregnancy is a lot on a healthy fit heart, so if you are starting at a less than optimal point, you must have a conversation with your doctor. Talk about things like a fast heart rate, slow heart rate, irregular heart rate, or a high or low blood pressure history. Discuss the type of monitoring that you will need, and when to come in, if you feel out of sorts. Yes, this includes if your monitor system at home is not working, and you feel unwell.

Knowing this changed the way I now think about my heart, and what I must do before baby arrives and afterward. Pregnancy is a huge heart stressor, especially if you had complications such as pre-eclampsia. As women, we need to always stay heart healthy by eating well and having an active lifestyle. We must make sure our follow-up medical appointments continue even after pregnancy.

I advocate every pregnant woman get a blood pressure machine that is calibrated by her provider. It is a valuable tool for monitoring your vitals. In a TED Talk presentation I listened to, the speaker estimated that pregnancy ages a woman's heart by 10-20 years, especially women who experience pre-eclampsia. They can later suffer from cardiac events, high blood pressure, or heart failure. Studies are being conducted to better understand these effects.

What can we do to stay heart healthy before, during, and after childbirth? Understand the stress of postpartum on the heart. Low sleep affects the heart. Stress up to two years affects the heart. Even child rearing can take a toll. Keep all that at the forefront.

I hope this information will influence your decision to stay heart healthy. Above all, don't take your body for granted. Instead, do your best to nurture it daily. Once baby arrives, please be vigilant. Conditions such as pre-eclampsia can occur up to six weeks after delivery and have effects up to a year. If you have a slow heart rate, and/or high blood pressure, chest pain, shortness of breath, or swelling, be sure to take those symptoms seriously and seek medical consultation.

Understanding the Maternal Death Numbers

"People can use fear to keep you stuck, it is up to you to learn to use fear to push through, to learn and to grow."
—Michelle Obama

Maternal mortality is your risk of dying as a mother during and after pregnancy, up to one-year postpartum.

It can be scary to hear information and not have a basis for what the numbers mean or refer to regarding your risk of dying during pregnancy. Especially when it flashes across your TV, in scary glaring red. The issue being that typically the context is never given, so if someone says 30% of our mothers are dying from something, you first have to pause and ask what that is referring to. Is it of the entire population, which is a much bigger number like in the millions or is it of people who died which is a much smaller number like in the tens or hundreds.

Reference can be everything. Form your own understanding of the numbers as they relate to maternal mortality rates, what they mean, and why there is concern.

First let's place the numbers in perspective. *Note: The following numbers are not exact and are rounded down for simplification:*

- According to the United States census bureau the total population of the US was approximately 329 million people in 2020.
- The population of women in the US aged 15-44 years of age was approximately 64 million people.
- In 2020 we had approximately 3.7 million live births- babies born with signs of life.

If nearly four million babies were born, how many women die from a preventable pregnancy-related cause during and up to a year after pregnancy? The number was 861.

The number seems small, but we must pay attention to what the number is doing. Is it going down or up? Especially considering medical advances and the United States being one of the wealthiest countries in the world.

Regarding maternal deaths, the United States currently ranks number 47. The number has been increasing since the seventies. In comparison, other countries are experiencing decreases in their maternal death rate.

Also, the United States' maternal death number is not the most alarming thing to note. Most frightening is that many women get hurt during pregnancy and delivery while suffering preventable complications. In 2020 approximately 50,000 women suffered pregnancy-related complications. These numbers are rising as well.

The United States is currently ranked number 59 in the world in terms of birthing outcomes.

What is my take on all of this? One preventable death of a mother is absolutely one too many. We must do everything in our power to stop these deaths from happening. Other high income earning countries are experiencing drops in their maternal death rates. The United States' maternal death rate is increasing. This should concern all of us—not only mothers.

Maternal Health Disparities for African American Women

Let's examine the troubling trends you may have heard about for African American women.

- There were 3.6 million babies delivered or live births in 2020.
- Out of those births 1.8 million were white, 529,811 babies were Black, 866,713 babies were Hispanic.
- Maternal mortality is represented per 100,000 live births which is a measure of how many women die due to pregnancy-related complications for every 100,000 babies born alive.
- In 2015, the maternal mortality rate for African Americans was 37.1 per 100,000 live births, compared to 11.4 for American Indians, 12.8 for Hispanics, 8.2 for Whites, and 9.7 for Asians.
- By 2023, the maternal mortality rate for African Americans increased to 40.2 per 100,000 live births, compared to 11.7 for American Indians, 12.7 for Hispanics, 8.0 for Whites, and 8.8 for Asians. This indicates that the maternal mortality rate for African Americans has been increasing over time, while the rates for other racial and ethnic groups have remained relatively stable.
- African American women are more likely to die due to pregnancy-related complications than any other group in the US, with 37 out of every 100,000 babies born alive to African American mothers dying before their first birthday.
- Maternal death rates have increased across the board for all races since 2018. However, based on smaller population size, the maternal death rate is greatest for black women.

- The percent chance of having maternal morbidity or mortality can vary between racial and ethnic groups. According to the Centers for Disease Control and Prevention, African American women are 3.3 times more likely to die from pregnancy-related complications than white women, and Hispanic women are 1.5 times more likely to die from pregnancy-related complications than white women. Asian women are 1.2 times more likely to die from pregnancy-related complications than white women.

In general, if a woman possesses a high level of education or socioeconomic status, she has a lower risk for problems during pregnancy. This is true for every group except black women. To place this in perspective, this means a black woman could hold a master's degree, live in a home worth more than $400,000, and earn more than $300,000 a year and she would still experience problems with pregnancy and delivery. Why is this? Well, evidence says that comorbidity may be a factor. What's even more troubling is that bias and racism may also play a role.

Disparities affect Native Americans and Latin communities as well, but the maternal mortality findings are more pronounced for black and white women hence why the focus of most of the research and data is on the majorities that are affected.

So why is this happening? Well, it's complex and below I share the most common researched reasons this may be happening more frequently for some than others. Some simple reasons offered are that we are collecting better data now than before so under reporting was an issue for hospitals, also we are having children later than before, so our advanced age is showing a concurrent increase in complications especially for minorities. But it doesn't explain the whole picture especially when compared to other countries.

History of chronic disease, heart disease: As shared earlier, pregnancy takes a toll on the body, therefore have any existing conditions especially those affecting the heart or risk for infection can increase your risk of fatal complications during pregnancy, being aware and working closely with your health care team is extremely important. Conditions such as obesity, diabetes, high blood pressure, heart conditions increase your risk. Sadly, these conditions occur more for women of color.

Training and experience of the health care team: Part of current efforts to improve maternal health have to do with addressing the gap in the way we manage the common complications in pregnancy. In the past every provider and hospital managed these conditions independently, leading to varying outcomes. Standardization will go a long way and using evidence-based practice in a collaborative way.

There are strong efforts to ensure the continued creation in all states of these standardized clinical managements, on conditions like blood clots, pre-eclampsia, etc.

We also don't routinely see these complications here in our country. Doctors are not trained to recognize and manage in a standard way some of these complications that they rarely encounter. My dad was an OB-GYN in Nigeria. In speaking with him and describing the care and education he received there, he said some of the complications we rarely see here were an everyday occurrence in his country. He talked about hospitals having wards dedicated specifically to rare conditions we see here, like eclampsia. He gave me insight that the numbers for complications like pre-eclampsia are very low in American. Most doctors here don't truly learn during their training how to diagnose or manage it. This can lead providers to miss the early or middle stage signs. Continuous education must be provided for rare high mortality diseases in pregnancy. My dad in his practice experienced the severe effects of lack of access, watching woman travel by foot hundreds to thousands of miles to receive care. I watched him in a care desert, caring for patients while long lines of mothers waited to be seen. I saw him receive payment in fruits and farm bounty as these patients didn't have anything to give financially. Most impactful where the ones my dad lost and the toll it took on him, mostly due to poor access or not getting to his hospital on time. I wonder what it would be like to have collaboration utilizing technological communications to perform virtual grand rounds with providers in other countries to help provide that education that we so obviously need here for these low volume ailments that are common in other countries.

Wrong patient, wrong hospital:

As a provider who has worked in several hospitals, I have always assumed that most hospitals operate at a certain level, in order words they should have certain types of specialists needed available 24/7, or equipment like an MRI or an echo, an ultrasound of the heart 24/7? I've taken this for granted because I have always lived and practiced in the city where most cities have this level of services routinely, but the experiences I went through during my pregnancy made me realize that all hospitals are not prepared to take care of all levels of patients even those that may appear to be large in name and size. I realized that it was important information for me to have, and it scared me that going to the wrong hospital could affect the care and more so the outcome.

The level of service that a hospital has, is not always readily transparent or clear, and it can be a source of risk to birthing persons. So much so that an initiative is underway as I write this to ensure that all hospitals that provide maternal care be transparent about the classification of service they provide and to ensure they have a clear plan to escalate or collaborate with a higher-level center if something goes wrong, they cannot handle. An organization called the joint commission ensures that hospitals maintain and practice high safety quality standards to result in zero harm to patients. Let me repeat that: zero harm. Yes, even one preventable death is completely unacceptable, and it takes these types of organizations that will hold these hospitals and centers accountable so that you can ensure your care is a priority not just in words but in process and action. It is helpful to know that this work is under way at the state and national level. But until then, you should know the levels and speak with your doctor to make sure that the hospital you are delivering in matches the level of your risk and that it is clear where you can be expected to be cared for if a higher level of care is needed. This care is not just for baby but for mom as well.

REASONS FOR DISADVANTAGES FOR AFRICAN AMERICAN WOMEN

According to research, some African American women are at a huge disadvantage when it comes to their risk of maternal mortality for these reasons:

1. Lack of access to healthcare: Black women are less likely to have access to quality healthcare due to financial, geographic, and cultural barriers.
2. Lack of insurance: Black women are more likely to be uninsured compared to other racial groups, making it difficult to access healthcare services.
3. Higher rates of chronic conditions: Black women are more likely to have chronic conditions such as diabetes and hypertension, which can lead to complications during pregnancy.
4. Higher rates of preterm birth: Black women are more likely to have preterm births, which can lead to an increased risk of infant mortality.
5. Higher risk of infection: Black women are more likely to have infections such as HIV and hepatitis B, which can lead to pregnancy complications.
6. Lack of education: Black women are less likely to have access to resources and information about pregnancy and childbirth.

7. Systemic racism: Structural racism can lead to disparities in healthcare, such as unequal access to quality care and treatment.

8. Socioeconomic factors: Black women are more likely to live in poverty, which can lead to a lack of access to resources and increased stress.

9. Trauma: Black women are more likely to have experienced trauma, which can lead to mental health issues that can affect pregnancy and childbirth.

10. Discrimination: Black women are more likely to experience discrimination in healthcare settings, which can lead to care that is not tailored to their needs. What causes this racism? Racism is caused by a combination of social, economic, and political factors. It is rooted in a history of systemic oppression and discrimination, including slavery and Jim Crow laws that have impacted access to resources and opportunities. Racism is also perpetuated by institutional policies and practices, as well as by individual attitudes and behaviors.

I was surprised to learn about new science indicating that certain life events all the way from childhood affect the brain. In other words, our brains can be hurt by more than we realize. This hurt sometimes is an attempt to repair itself, but we tend to not consider the effects of most situations on this amazing organ.

Research shows chronic stress may damage the area of the brain called the prefrontal cortex which can affect executive functions, including tasks like strategizing, future planning, organizing, controlling impulsivity. When I think of that child who lost its mother at a young age, or witnessed or received emotional or verbal abuse… who then becomes an adult who is also routinely a victim of bias, racial discrimination, or witnessing their loved ones or community being on the receiving end… yes, the woman does not have to actually be the direct receiver, witnessing or having it happen to someone else can create the same stress effects. More surprising was how these effects can lead to behaviors that may increase the risk for chronic diseases, hypertension, diabetes, substance abuse, and so on.

Bias and racism especially over time can be very stressful and can increase a mother's risk for complications and bad outcomes, not just psychologically but also physically.

Picture that woman of color who possibly from childhood or even young adulthood was on the receiving end of chronic stress, and then is a victim of racial discrimination in a hospital setting. Research shows her health outcomes can be drastically affected. Her risk for pre-eclampsia rises. Why is it important to know this? Doctors, nurses, family members—it is important for all of us to know about the risk for issues during pregnancy. If we have been stressed, we may need to anticipate more support from the get-go, support like therapy, mindfulness, talking with loved ones and yes communicating your stress history to your clinician to help.

Mama, are you juggling just one hectic job or three jobs and a pregnancy? Supporting a sick parent while being pregnant? These sources of chronic stress can affect your health outcomes. I hope for a world where providers help their patients anticipate needing additional support within their clinical networks such as a social worker or even a doula to support and manage stressful situations involving bias or discrimination.

Leading Maternal Death Issues

"There is something about losing a mother that is permanent and inexpressible—a wound that will never quite heal."
—Susan Wiggs

Dear mama, I don't know when our time will end on this beautiful planet, but I hope your end will never be for a pointless reason. Especially not for a preventable situation such as being dismissed or ignored during your maternal health journey.

Fellow mothers, we have power. Our power starts with knowledge. Knowledge of the biggest risks to our lives when we enter our motherhood journey.

While writing this chapter, the voices of past clinical mentors and colleagues echoed in my head, saying, "Too much information is a bad thing. Women won't know what to do with it. They will think they have everything you listed, and they will call the clinic everyday wondering if they have that or this."

Let me unpack this more.

With so much information available via the Internet, daily, clinicians meet patients who have researched their diagnosis ahead of time. Sometimes women have printed out pages of what they think might happen with their bodies.

During my training and to this very day I will see clinicians roll their eyes, their body language stating the following,

"Ugh! Not another person looking at WebMD thinking the worst is going on with them!"

Or,

"Did that person go to medical school?"

Or,

"How dare they question my authority!"

Still, some would smile and take the time to review the concerns and say why or how their symptoms didn't fit what they saw on WebMD. These varied reactions have intrigued me for some time now.

Our access to information is increasing whether or not we like it. My challenge to all my fellow clinicians is to encourage that curiosity, especially if it can save a life. Rather, channel it— use it as a conversation starter and collaboration.

Mama, I give you permission to figure out what may ail you. Even if your research leads you down the wrong path, that is not the worst thing that can happen to you. If what you read or hear helps you better explain what is worrying you, then it's up to the healthcare team to listen and work with you to plan a diagnosis. The team should investigate the likely or not so likely culprit of your pain and other symptoms through a physical and investigatory work up.

I once had a conversation with an OB-GYN briefly after graduate school. By that time, I had medical knowledge, and I realized, based on my symptoms, I needed to discuss my fertility concerns with her.

When I walked into the exam room, I was nervous. I never thought I had the power to question my doctor. Rather, I passively answered questions and let my doctor tell me what was wrong. I offered little unless I was asked. It was like I thought if I offered or talked too much, then something bad would be diagnosed. I thought less conversation or interaction was better. In short, I left my power outside of the room.

On that day, I asked because I knew I really wanted to have kids. My lips trembled as I spoke, "Dr. so and so, I'm sorry to bother but I think I may have PCOS, and I'm nervous it could affect my chance to get pregnant."

She stared at me for what seemed like an uncomfortably long moment, then she laughed out loud, startling me.

"Silly, you don't look like a PCOS patient," she said. "I'll see you next year."

She walked out, and I left the room feeling stupid for having questioned her authority.

Fast forward ten years after that visit. This time I perched in the room of a reputable fertility specialist. Again, I visited to find out why I had been unsuccessful getting pregnant.

He walked into the room with test results in hand. "You have classic PCOS," he said.

Next, he showed me all the findings from my hormone levels to the cysts on my ultrasound.

Floored, I stared past him and remembered my visit ten years earlier with that other lady and I was mad at myself that I didn't know how to advocate for myself. Steaming that I didn't possess the skills to present questions or have a dialogue with my doctor — one that was collaborative, not top down.

I had not been taught, nor did I ever learn communication skills for my role as a patient. I didn't know what I should bring to the table to ensure my best health outcome.

We must teach our children their role as patients. We must teach our providers, hospital staff their role and the role of the patient, to ensure we no longer ascribe to the ancient "doctor knows best" paradigm. Together, both the patient and doctor know best because they work together to arrive at the best solution suited to the patient.

In order to help your healthcare team, you should have a basic understanding of the top ten things that can harm or kill you while pregnant. Learn their names, symptoms, and frequency because you are the captain of the ship. You will be the first person to feel that something is wrong with your body, because you understand when you feel good. Trust yourself. When you feel off-course, it is time to seek answers. Trust your intuition and use your awareness in a non-fear motivated way. Embrace a sense of empowerment through preparation.

As you learn about the most common killers of moms, use it as a place to start powerful conversations with your healthcare team, and to better understand your risk. This is not an exhaustive list, just enough to help you gain awareness and start a conversation. It's hard to tell when things go wrong in pregnancy because many women feel terrible at baseline. Concerns can be easily dismissed as typical symptoms of pregnancy.

Knowing your physical feelings at baseline and listening to your gut when those feelings change can be the difference between life and death.

Hypertensive Disorders

Hypertensive disorders (such as pre-eclampsia or eclampsia) are still being studied. However, research points to the attachment of the placenta as being one of the hallmarks. The most important thing to realize is that your risk for pre-eclampsia after baby is born continues past the six-week mark. Be vigilant with your health care team and report if your blood pressure is higher than your usual numbers.

Work very closely with your medical team to determine your risk, and whether or not you should take any preventive measures (such as taking a baby aspirin daily in your second trimester). Your medical team can decide what numbers indicate that you should seek care, considering the following:

- For your heart rate, if it is too slow (less than 60 beats per minute), or too fast (over 100 beats per minute).

- For your breathing, we call the oxygen saturation or 02 sat if less than 95%.
- For your blood pressure—if the systolic or top number is consistently greater than 150 and the bottom number or diastolic number is over 100 seek immediate care. If numbers combined with severe headache, changes in your vision, trouble breathing, and abdominal pain. Please discuss what an abnormal blood pressure is for you based on your usual, as a lower systolic than above may be concerning for you.

Having pre-eclampsia increases your risk later in life of having kidney disease, heart disease, high blood pressure, and stroke, so maintain a healthy lifestyle and keep up with routine follow-ups to monitor yourself.

CARDIOMYOPATHY

Cardiomyopathy refers to a situation when the muscle of the heart becomes affected and doesn't pump blood well to the rest of the body. This eventually can cause the heart to fail. Signs can be trouble breathing, swelling of legs, ankle and feet, tiredness, fluttering heartbeat, chest pressure, dizziness, or fainting.

INFECTION OR SEPSIS

Maternal sepsis was the second leading cause of death between 2014 and 2017. It can occur during and sometimes up to 6 weeks or more after delivery. Sepsis is caused by an infection somewhere in the body (such as in the lung), pneumonia, or a urinary tract infection (UTI). The infection kicks off a large inflammatory response in the body and causes organ dysfunction or failure. Other causes are miscarriage, C-section, prolonged labor, or mastitis infection in the breast. According to the Center for Disease Control, additional risks include never having given birth before, and mothers of multiples, having a history diabetes, and being African American. The best cure is early recognition of symptoms: fast heart rate, dizziness, change in your blood pressure especially if lower, and frequent urination from a UTI.

If you think you may have an infection or sepsis, stay vigilant and escalate any concerns by going straight to the hospital or calling 911. Simply say, "I am concerned I might have sepsis."

PULMONARY EMBOLISM

When pregnant, you are up to five times more likely to develop a blood clot because of the effect a large uterus has on the blood flow to the lower legs, as well as increased production of blood clotting factors.

When a clot forms in the leg, it can travel to the lungs and cause a pulmonary embolism. Recognizing the symptoms early and being aware of your history is important. For example, tennis champion Serena Williams recognized and self-advocated for her blood clot symptoms and got started on blood thinner medications. However, symptoms can be vague, so it is important every pregnant woman know the signs and be alert.

Look for pain or swelling that is worse and more noticeable in one leg compared to the other. Dizziness, fainting, increased heart rate, or unexplained anxiety, we call it impending doom a feeling some report when they have a blood clot.

You may be at risk for blood clots if:

- You are over 35 years old, or have had surgery on your bone or joint, or of any kind.
- You are recovering after a C-section or any surgery. Since you can't move, high compressed stockings are placed on your legs to reduce your risk of blood clotting. Gently squeeze your leg to keep the blood

moving. Ask for compression stockings if your provider has not given them to you.

- You are obese, on extended bed rest, or if you have not moved for long periods of time.
- You have traveled extendedly or if you live a sedentary lifestyle, have cancer, or have sickle cell disease.

Let your doctor and team know if you have had a history of PE or in your family. Your medical team can use an ultrasound, CAT scan, or blood work to check for this. You may qualify if you have had a history of using low dose blood thinner during and after pregnancy. As always, talk frankly with your doctor to decide what is best.

AMNIOTIC FLUID EMBOLISM

Amniotic fluid embolism is extremely rare. Only one in 40,000 may have an allergic reaction to amniotic fluid. Risks include advanced maternal (older than 35 years), expecting multiples, pre-eclampsia, or having a C-section.

An amniotic fluid embolism is also very hard to detect. Symptoms may be sudden and include, difficulty breathing, sudden drop in your blood pressure, abnormal heart rate, bleeding from uterus or incision site, confusion, anxiety, and chills.

HEMORRHAGE

A hemorrhage is bleeding from damaged blood vessels, which can occur internally or externally. There are several reasons you may experience bleeding, such as an issue with the position or implantation of the placenta during pregnancy, or incomplete removal of the placenta after delivery.

Speak with your doctor about the type of bleeding to worry

about and when you should come in. In general, any bleeding that lasts over two hours should be brought to the attention of your health care team. Seek immediate care if you have abdominal pain or any other symptoms such as low blood pressure, fainting, and / or fever.

Suicide, Postpartum Depression, and Psychosis

We forget the effects pregnancy and its hormonal changes can have on the brain. Sadly, this is on the rise according to the research. Suicide is being described as a leading cause of maternal mortality. Most at risk per the literature are women with mental health diagnosis and substance abuse disorders, history of traumatic birth experiences, low support, stressful pregnancy, prior history of postpartum depression. Mental health screenings but also awareness for mom and also family members to be on alert and provide support is imperative.

One of the biggest things to monitor is sleep. Be vigilant of just how much sleep mama is getting. Lack of sleep can worsen symptoms and increase risk for psychosis. Sleep deprivation can be dangerous for moms with mental health symptoms. Sleep training, and support with a doula or night nurse to allow mom to sleep can go a long way. Also, pressure to breast feed if not able, and stopping anti-depressant medications, due to fear of affecting baby could contribute to psychosis. Be vigilant for symptoms up to one year postpartum. They include intrusive thoughts, of self-harm, or harm to baby or children, feelings of shame and not being a wonderful mom, or not feeling *like other moms.*

Often, moms don't share feelings because they fear the worst, which is someone taking their children. So, they suffer in silence. Journaling from the beginning of pregnancy is encouraged to get thoughts out. Confide in a trusted loved one with whom you have had a pre-pregnancy conversation to help escalate your care when you may not feel like talking. Therapy, peer support groups, medications can be so helpful. You never have to feel alone.

Postpartum psychosis is different from postpartum blues or depression or anxiety, it is a rare but serious mental health disorder that can occur in the days or weeks after giving birth even up to a year. Symptoms of postpartum psychosis include extreme confusion, disorientation, delusions, hallucinations, paranoia, and suicidal thoughts. If a mother is experiencing any of these symptoms, it is important to call 911 and seek immediate medical care, mother must have 24/7 supervision at all times until cleared by a licensed mental health professional. Continuous supervision is emphasized, no mini periods unsupervised.

The risk of suicide and infanticide with postpartum psychosis is very high and should be taken seriously. Again, seek immediate medical attention if any of the symptoms of postpartum psychosis are present.

Create a safe environment for mama and baby and provide support and resources to help manage the symptoms always under the supervision of a mental health provider.

If you are pregnant and high-risk plan to deal with signs of psychosis by educating yourself about the disorder, seeking professional help from a mental health provider, and creating a safety plan.

- Seek out community resources, creating a routine, and engaging in activities that can help reduce stress.
- Create a support network of family and friends
- Engage in regular physical activity • eating a balanced diet • practicing relaxation techniques
- Avoid triggers such as substance use and stress
- Create as much as possible a calm space for the mother to rest and relax

STROKE AND CEREBRAL VASCULAR INCIDENTS

Pregnancy is a huge heart and vascular system stressor, and it can increase your risk of stroke. Pregnancy elevates your risk of having a very high blood pressure, blood clots, pre-eclampsia, and eclampsia.

Symptoms are headaches, which may be confused if you typically have migraines. Other symptoms are confusion, trouble walking, lack of balance, or lack of coordination. If having pain, weakness, numbness to one arm, more weakness in your face or slurred speech, call 911 immediately. Don't drive. You can reduce your risk by staying active, working with your team to treat your diabetes or high blood pressure, eat healthy foods, and no smoking.

If you think someone may have a stroke, act F.A.S.T. and do the following test:

- **F** —Face: Ask the person to smile. Does one side of the face droop?
- **A** —Arms: Ask the person to raise both arms. Does one arm drift downward?
- **S** —Speech: Ask the person to repeat a simple phrase. Is the speech slurred or strange?
- **T** —Time: If you see any of these signs, call 9-1-1 right away.

Note the time when any symptoms first appear. This information helps health care providers determine the best treatment for each person.

THE COST OF MATERNAL MORTALITY

"A mother is she who can take the place of all others but whose place no one else can take."
—Cardinal Meymillod

THE POWERFUL EFFECT WOMEN, especially mothers, have on society is routinely taken for granted. It is often unappreciated or dismissed in scenarios we can all recount. In this section, I hope to shed light on the astronomical value of women.

We cannot tolerate or accept another preventable death for moms. I hope that in showing the value that we lose when a mom dies or is absent it will inspire you to do your part in joining the ongoing efforts to fight the disparities that exist.

Children need their mothers to increase their risk for not just survival in this world but also thriving, when a mother is lost the threat of survival to the child is not only at stake but also the quality of life, their physical and psychological health, socioeconomic power, education of the child, and also the family, community, nation, and even future generations according to the literature. In the short term, the greatest risk are families breaking up to ensure survival of the children and economic difficulties.

Here are a few areas that are affected in the long run.

Economy

The income lost after a mother dies can be hard to recover which can lead to several things happening to the children, to improve their survival they may be sent away to live with other relatives to maximize financial resources, the emotional toll of not having present birth parents can be significant.

Women invest and support others. Talk to any mother and follow her finances and you will most likely see that her finances no matter how big or small their status goes to supporting more than just her immediate family, it's her friends, church, community, coworkers. Women spend their hard-earned finances and time on so many others as they invest in family and their communities.

Think about the carpool efforts that allow other moms to provide for their families and contribute to the economy. Children receive snacks and lunches given by other mothers when they may not get them from their own family. Programs are influenced by a mother's ability to encourage creativity, advocacy, and team building. The list goes on and on. A healthy mother shows her children and their friends, "Yes, you can do it!". Follow a wonderful mother and you will see the reach and impact that only one person has in making this world so much better.

Thriving mothers help support and build incredible communities.

Family Survival

When a mother dies suddenly, some fathers left behind cannot cope and support the household in the way the mother did. Women, according to the literature, have a greater capacity to perform a multitude of tasks while running a home. Research speculates that, in the long term, children affected by maternal mortality may search for emotional and financial support and enter early or insecure relationships. These relationships may also perpetuate their future risk for maternal mortality, as unstable unions may fail, leading to multiple relationships with children from each—this is a direct link to a low socioeconomic status.

Emotional and Physical Health of Child and Community

When a mother dies shortly after birth, the nutritional status of the surviving children may be affected. If you are a mother, think about how much attention you pay to the food your child eats and whether or not they eat. Also, when a mother is gone, grief and the financial strain may create stress short term but also long term. Stress from the absence may be speculated to cause long-term risks for chronic disease, substance abuse, and morbidity.

Community Building

When a woman says she is becoming a stay-at-home mom or working part time, it can bring on assumptions both by family and her workplace co-workers. Even if she is truly working hard at home and doing her part, self-doubt can creep in because of the title: stay-at-home mom. However, a mother's contributions far extend beyond the home. Those contributions should be celebrated just as much as the title of a working mom. Research shows that nurturing mothers and fathers increase the chance for children who go on to financial independence, good citizenship, and stable emotional maturity.

Intergenerational Education

Mothers typically spend a great deal of time and resources on managing the education of their child in school and in the home. A dedicated mother assists with a child's focus, increasing the likelihood that the child will connect with the educational material enough to do well on the test.

After losing a mom, statistics indicate that children may have difficulty concentrating and even successfully completing higher education because of emotional stress and lack of finances. When mom is missing, older siblings often become caretakers of their younger siblings or do more chores to support their own households. Children can struggle to balance home responsibilities with school, which may lead to poor performance in school, struggling and even dropping out. Incomplete education can feed the poverty cycle for generations. Engaged and financially stable and supportive guardians or surrogate parents may help reduce these outcomes.

What Do We Lose When a Mother Dies?

In my studies, and personal experiences, I realized that it was impossible to quantify the loss of a mother. Whenever I reflect on the absence of my mom, or losing my friend, or the life of my grandmother, I shudder to think of what those losses cost our communities.

As a society, we have not been taught to appreciate the value of mothers and the incredible loss losing just one can cause.

It is not just the grief felt in the family, but in the local and international communities for generations to come.

A mother is not only responsible for nurturing a child. She is part of major society nurturing and advocacy efforts. Think of the unbelievable mothers, grandmothers, great grandmothers in your life. Imagine if any of them had lost their life in a preventable way during or after childbirth. Imagine all their accomplishments never having happened. My grandmother would never have started colleges and allowed free education for thousands of students in her lifetime who provided for their families.

In her brief life, my friend Liz performed incredible support and outreach for her community through education, hospitality, advocacy for colorectal cancer, emotional support for friends, family. Losing Liz had ripple effects beyond her immediate family to her community, city, and nation.

WHAT IS BEING DONE?

"Change will not come if we wait for some other person or some other time. We are the ones we've been waiting for. We are the change that we seek."
 -Barack Obama

HEALTHCARE IN AMERICA has come a long way. Today, some people are fortunate to have access to advances and technologies that didn't exist thirty years ago.

Though the healthcare continuum is slow to change, developments for the better are on the way. I hope this helps you to expect wonderful work in the future. Some of you can see it already with amazing programs, campaigns, and laws meant to ensure mothers are kept safer than they are now.

While working with your provider, you must still be the captain of your amazing body. You'll work alongside them, not under them, to educate yourself, especially if something goes wrong. Though emergencies are rare, you must still understand your risk.

Below, I summarize what is being done in the United States to fight for positive changes in maternal health. There is so much that I still don't know. So many amazing individuals, groups, and organizations that I'm barely scratching the surface.

The most exciting areas I am looking towards for reform and improvement are access for all to have improved access to quality maternity care and robust educations during medical training for healthcare providers to learn skills to see and hear all patients regardless of their race, economic status and more.

I look forward to racial and equity and communication courses becoming second place not just in training but continuously being reinforced like cardiopulmonary resuscitation (CPR) courses that save lives but also realize that the skills need to be reinforced and clinician held accountable. I hope one day that classes that teach communication, implicit bias and racism prevention are required annually to reinforce and over time hone and grow these skills and undo decades of hard-wired beliefs that clinicians consciously or unconsciously bring to their practice.

Doctors and all other healthcare providers alone cannot provide care to the millions of women requiring maternal care. Burnout rates and our current systems don't allow our providers consistent success while providing care. I believe that, over time, we will continue to feel the effects of maternal care deserts requiring an assortment of well-coordinated maternal health providers. Providers who would collaborate to educate each other—to support the beautiful ecosystem that is our mothers giving birth to our future generations. OB-GYN doctors supporting midwives, doulas, community health partners and advocates all working together to provide amazing care.

Over thirty congressional bills have been introduced in response to the increasing maternal mortality rates. These legislature changes target improvements to the maternal health care system landscape.

Though it will take time, I hope you find peace knowing many incredibly dedicated individuals are passionate in their fight for better maternal care. These people are currently fighting for:

- Significant efforts to assemble task forces including maternal health workers, community organizations, patient experience representatives and so much more to improve care for vulnerable populations such as Black, indigenous, and other people of color (BIPOC), veterans, incarcerated, and others.
- Provide funding for digital tools, including telehealth, to improve the outcomes of maternal health especially in underserved areas.
- Improve funding to better support moms with mental health conditions and substance abuse disorders.
- Advance respectful maternity care in the future and consider the unique caveats for pregnancy in dealing with COVID-19.
- Transformation of our healthcare systems by creating standardization and best practice especially for the common killers, improving health care coordination, maternity health home financing, improve transition in and out of pregnancy, patient centered care, ensure equity is integrated into all quality efforts.
- Standardize the data collection of maternal morbidity and mortality events, improve access to culturally competent care, pay for doula support services, expand Medicaid coverage to new moms for one year postpartum.
- Expand the maternal health workforce to improve address maternal health care deserts. By offering reimbursement for doulas, night nurses, midwives, and so on.
- Implicit bias training and skills testing for all health care providers especially those in maternal health specialty.

- Increased accountability by governing bodies like joint commission to make sure hospitals are doing the right thing performing routine trainings to ensure competence.
- Create a transparent designation for the quality and level of care that maternal health centers provide, so that individuals can make their own decision about the best place for time. Designations such as "birthing friendly" are on their way and signify if a center has met the standards of governing bodies of consistently providing safe care.

PART TWO

THE POWER OF SAVING YOURSELF

Understanding The Importance of Your Medical Story

"Stories can take away dignity and stories can restore dignity."
—Chimamanda Ngozi Adichie

I'M FASCINATED with storytelling and always will be. It continues to be a big part of my career in medicine and coaching. I have been fortunate to hear so many stories not just of people's medical conditions but their families, hopes, dreams, fears and more. As well so many of my patients have asked for my life stories.

Whenever I perform a procedure on a patient, such as placing a catheter in their vein to deliver cancer medication, I often use the opportunity to listen to their stories. Patients offer me insight into their worlds. I always felt privileged that in the short time of meeting me, my patients would trust me enough to talk about their personal histories. Though many of them differed from me in race, age, and gender, within those brief moments we always connected when they talked about family, faith, fears, hopes, and dreams. Our differences didn't matter.

Working in emergency medicine meant performing under tight time constraints. However, I still needed to help my patients tell their medical stories. Whenever I talked with them, my goal was to deduce and make an educated guess regarding what might be wrong. I also needed to determine what needed further evaluation through labs and imaging. I had to reach the core of what brought that patient to the emergency room. It was rare that it was ever one big thing. Most people had something concerning them, but they also had also chronic issues they had not had time to seek care for, so they would use that opportunity to share all the concerns.

Several times, the issues the patient shared turned out not to be the most urgent thing pressing them. Some patients don't have the skills to communicate clearly about their medical concerns. However, the way they tell their story, their tone, what is said or not said, can affect how the provider manages their care.

How a patient tells their story is extremely important.

Understanding what your body feels like under normal circumstances and then realizing there has been a change—your ability to communicate that can mean the difference between life and death. Going one step forward to guide your care team is extremely helpful.

Though it is the health provider's responsibility to ask the correct questions, remember this is a shared responsibility. You have all the information. Your provider can help you more when they understand more about your history. In addition, your health history is a shared responsibility with your loved ones who can share your medical background on your behalf.

I remember witnessing colleagues whose patients returned, even though when we looked at the case again, there were obvious signs in hindsight that they should not have been sent home. Or, that they should have been admitted. The patient with appendicitis symptoms. The patient with chest pain. The situations weren't always related to the competence of the provider. Did the mistake occur because of the story that was told? Did the provider feel they had an unconscious permission to minimize the complaints the patient was presenting with?

When you don't tell your medical story accurately, clinicians can take the wrong approach with your care, or dismiss the main reason you came to the hospital.

It takes a very skilled provider to help a patient focus and ask the right questions to gather necessary information to deduce if there are any alarming ailments going on with the patient. Bias may play a role in how effective your story is heard. Statistics show that black children and adults may be less likely to be admitted or even be classified as having a need for emergency care.

You must tell your story clearly.

This chapter will teach you how to persist if you feel ignored or dismissed. You will learn the framework every medical provider uses to gather your story. Understanding it can help you prepare and organize your story with little room for misunderstanding.

It is important to gain insight into the standard information most healthcare providers will ask of you, so that you can be prepared and can organize your thoughts. Remember, this is a *framework*. You may not need to follow it word for word, but you can base your answers on the sample questions. The provider will tailor what question comes next.

ANATOMY OF THE MEDICAL HISTORY

Every clinician follows a similar framework when trying to get your medical story, though there may be slight differences based on the specialty. A provider may ask more or less of a particular area, and so on, such as when you seek maternal health care.

This chapter will teach you how to tell your health history in an emergency. Time may be limited depending on how busy the hospital or clinic is, and you may feel rushed. It can help to have some awareness. While waiting, think about your medical story.

Use your journal, the one that already includes your past medical story, to avoid getting flustered. Since you are not feeling well, you may even be frustrated at some questions. Being prepared can go a long way, especially with answers that force you to recall things that happened a long time ago (for example, when was your first period). Being asked that question when you are complaining of eight out of ten pain can make even the most patient person irritated and literally want to scream, especially remember these questions may need to be asked several times by every provider and health care team you see.

Yes, you will have to repeat your story. I know it can frustrate you. It may seem like the doctors and nurses are not talking to one another.

REASONS PROVIDERS ASK SIMILAR QUESTIONS

Medical staff must document all their encounters with you. The nurse, the intern or trainee or medical student may also if in an academic setting use the opportunity to practice getting your history, the resident, the nurse practitioner, the physician associate, and the doctor, of any new specialty you meet. In some ways an electronic record helps, but if you are new most people do their notes later in the day so these questions are a big part of our assessment and so we need to ask them individually to document later but do our own assessment, think of it as also fact checking; you don't want someone to have written the wrong thing and then everyone else keeps using incorrect information.

For different providers, parts of your story will trigger other types of question to ultimately get to the root of the problem. I have seen instances where the story changes based on who and how it is asked, so having sometime when you are feeling well to have answered and written your story can be very helpful, you can save this in a note section of your file or a health journal you take with you.

Imagine you had your full story written in your journal much earlier or even while waiting to be seen. Visualize that you already have it out and are ready to tell your story. Doesn't that sound better than having to remember your information while you are uncomfortable and unwell?

.

Telling Your Medical Story

"A woman doesn't need to find a voice, she has a voice, she needs to feel empowered to use it and people need to be encouraged to listen."
—Meghan Markle

LET'S dive into the main parts of your medical story that you want to have written and readily available. This chapter includes the question framework you'll receive when you see a medical provider—especially at a facility you've never visited, such as an emergency center or hospital.

Please note, this is not an exhaustive list. Depending on your situation, more or fewer questions may be asked.

What Should I Do with the Information?

First, use the content in this chapter to write out answers to all the important sections and questions.

Second, create a copy of your medical story to share with your spouse, partner, family member, or a support person. If needed, the designated person can then share your history with the healthcare team on your behalf.

Third, keep a copy of your medical story inside whatever purse or bag you would use when you go to a doctor's appointment or if you have to visit the emergency room or urgent care.

Your Medical History

List your full medical history. Medical providers typically want to know any other diagnosis you've experienced, or that you manage or take medicine to handle. You must share any chronic medical issues, such as diabetes, cancer, or heart disease.

Be detailed. Do not leave anything out about prior illnesses. Medical teams use this information to scan for patterns or clues that something has worsened or is leading to something else. For example, if you mention diabetes, your provider may ask if your sugar levels have been low or high—so make sure you list your recent blood sugar numbers.

If you've experienced several diagnoses, and are managing more than one, list them all along with the date/year (roughly) when you were diagnosed. Are they resolved now? Do you still take medication for these issues?

Your past mental health history is extremely important. Be honest about any mental health diagnosis requiring medication (for example, Prozac). Also, list anything that might block your ability to communicate your history, as your provider may need to rely on your family for detailed information.

History Statement Examples

"I have diabetes. I was diagnosed in 2004 during my second pregnancy. I take insulin daily."

"I have a doctor (your doctor's name and contact information should be noted in your journal) who provides my prescription (name the medication)."

"I have type 2 diabetes. I was diagnosed in 2018. My sugar

levels have been on the high side for the past month. I've listed my numbers in this journal."

"I've been diagnosed with clinical depression. I have never been hospitalized. I am under the care of a licensed psychiatrist, but I do not take medication."

List Your Allergies

Know and name your allergies. Medication allergies (for example, medications like penicillin). Food allergies. Animal or pet dander allergies. Mention any symptoms that occur when you have an allergic reaction — rash, swelling, difficulty breathing, eyes that swell shut.

List Your Surgery/Major Procedure History

Have you ever had surgery or a major medical procedure? List every surgery/procedure and the dates. As you get older, it's difficult to recall this information, so consider having a loved one help you talk about past medical procedures. In an emergency, a provider may only ask for surgeries that have to do with your chief complaint. They may not care about your bunion removal surgery but list it anyway. Share any issues with anesthesia or medication allergies, or any trouble you've had with pain medication.

List Your Sexual and Obstetrics History

Use a page of your journal to list vital sexual health history. You'll want to answer the following questions:
- When was your first period?
- When was your last period (first day of bleeding)?
- Do you experience heavy bleeding?
- Do you have fibroids?
- Do you bleed between cycles or during sex?

- How often do you have sex? What is your sexual orientation?
  - Do you use contraception? What type?
  - History of STDs?
  - When was your last pap smear?
  - How many children have you had (living and deceased)?
  - How many pregnancies, miscarriages, or abortions?
  - Have you experienced postpartum depression or anxiety?
  - Pregnancy complications? C-sections?
  - History of infertility? Infertility treatments or IVF?

List Your Immunizations History

Write your immunization record. List when you received your last shots for COVID-19, flu, tetanus (TDAP) and the rest.

List Your Family Medical History

Some diseases can be genetic, so note any medical diagnosis your parents, siblings, and grandparents have. Cancer. Heart disease. Be specific. If you have visited the medical facility in the past, the facility will have your info. If not, then yes, the organization needs this information.

Write Your Relationship History, Social History, and Job History

Medical providers like to know something about your social situations. Marital status. Job status. They want to make sure certain situations are not playing a role in your condition. They will ask if you are married, single, divorced, or if your situation is complicated.

Share your job history briefly. Focus on what you do currently. Be sure to include if you've worked in a factory or a location that may have exposed you to something.

Your education level is also important. Providers need to understand how well you can comprehend certain issues.

State your nationality and your religion or faith. Are there any special allowances needed for your care based on this? Or perhaps there are conditions local to your region you are from.

Do you smoke? How much? Do you drink alcohol? How much? Do you or have you ever done drugs? You will not get into trouble. Please be honest. You may have organ damage from using substances frequently.

Your nurse will ask your travel history in the last month, to make sure you didn't catch a bug while visiting a foreign region.

Also, if you don't feel safe at home, or have any concerns, a social worker can be provided to help. Talk with the nurse privately if you feel unsafe and that person will help you. Nurses are trained to check for signs—many are trained to discreetly ask your spouse to fill something out while they give you a chance to share if you need help. Be open with your social situation so you can get assistance. For example, information like being homeless, or a single mom with no childcare is good for your provider to know. A nurse can connect you with a social worker to help coordinate your care.

LIST YOUR MEDICATIONS

List any prescription medications you take by name, how much, how often, and the date when you started taking them. Do you take supplements over the counter which don't require a prescription? Write those down. Sometimes supplements cause medical issues. Be thorough. You will be so glad to pull this up and not have to recall this when you are not feeling well.

DETAIL YOUR CHIEF COMPLAINT

Whenever you seek care for a problem, while waiting to be seen, get clear on the reason(s) you came to get care.

We call this your chief complaint. A chief complaint is the main thing you came to seek care for, especially when you visit the ER.

- What are your symptoms?
- Are you in pain?
- Do you have a strange bodily feeling?
- Does your heart skip beats?
- Do you notice swelling?
- Did you pass out or feel light-headed?

List each symptom and clarify it. When did your issue start? Did it come and go? Was it constant? Did something make it better or worse? Did you take medicine for it? Did eating food or drinking water help the issue or make it worse?

If there is more than one symptom, list them all. For example, for chest pain, assign the pain a number, out of ten, with ten being the worst pain you have ever had. State what your pain tolerance is like and how this pain feels. Be clear on how it feels. Did you take something over the counter to help? If so, did it make you feel better?

CHIEF MEDICAL COMPLAINT EXAMPLES

- "I am here because I am having chest pain. I have never had this before and I am worried. The pain is right here (point to where it is and share if it moves side-to-side or front to back). The pain feels like pressure. It is not sharp. It feels like something is heavy and sitting on it. When I get it, it is a 9/10 pain. It makes me sweat, and I feel like I want to throw up."
- "I am here because I feel very sad. I am not usually feeling this way. I cry all the time. I don't want to get out of bed. I don't want to hold my baby. My family said that this is very different as well, and they are concerned."

- "I am here because I am concerned about the swelling in my hands, feet, and face. I know pregnant women can experience swelling, but my friends and family are concerned they have never seen swelling this bad. I am also concerned about this and need to make sure it is checked."
- "I'm here because I am forgetting a lot. My family said they speak to me, and I don't remember talking to them. I forget to feed my baby and do things around the house. I am concerned. This is unusual for me."
- HOW TO COMMUNICATE YOUR CHIEF COMPLAINT IF YOU ARE NOT FEELING AS SICK AS YOU DID WHEN YOU TRAVELED TO THE ER: "I am here because I have been having severe headaches. That is unusual for me. It started two days ago, and it wakes me up from my sleep. I get nausea with it, and I get dizzy. The pain comes and goes. My last episode was at 1:00 AM and was severe. That was what brought me to urgent care. The pain occurs every few hours. I am very concerned about it, and I need to be checked."

I hope these examples give you ideas of how to share your chief complaint. Remember, your clinical picture can change while you are waiting to be seen. It does not mean you no longer need care. The doctor or nurse will then ask more based on what you share.

LEVERAGE YOUR MEDICAL STORY

The previous information is a blueprint. It is a tool for you to prepare so that you can be clear when telling your story. When you present with a concern, especially to an emergent setting because something feels wrong, your provider will ask questions and your story provides the answers. The provider organizes your answers in such a way as to form a theory about what could occur. This happens before gathering more detailed data from labs and imaging.

For example, if you come in complaining of abdominal pain, providers will want to know:

- When did it start?
- Where is it?
- Is it in one place or does it move around?
- What is the quality of the pain? Sharp? Cramping? Dull?

ACT IF YOU ARE NOT HEARD

Be specific if conversations grow heated, or you try to talk about a serious issue and you feel tuned out.

Say something like, "I am very concerned about XXX. Also, my family is concerned. Can you share what workup you will do to make sure it is addressed? "

Repeat back what the provider says to make sure you understand. For example, "you said that for my headache you will check my blood pressure, check my urine, and do a blood test. Did I understand that?"

Or you can try, "I'm frustrated and very concerned about X. Can you share how you will address Y?"

After talking to your medical provider, thank them for addressing your concern. Breathe. The provider is not your enemy. Even if your trust level is low, your main goal is to be heard. Help the provider care for you.

YOUR PHYSICAL AND MENTAL EXAMINATION

So, you have done your note taking as we have talked about and written your history, so you don't have to be stressed by recalling your full life of medical history. You also clearly shared the main reason you left home to seek care. You have made your concerns clear.

Now what?

The provider must examine you based on your symptoms. The doctor or healthcare provider will survey your body for signs that may pinpoint your issue.

Note that while you shared your history, the provider observed you. Providers pick up on a lot of things as you talk. Are you short of breath? Agitated? Calm? Wincing? Appearing light-headed? Observation is a large part of the exam. Again, based on your history, your exam may be focused on general areas of concern. For example, if you have leg pain and swelling, the medical team will inspect your extremities.

The medical center should always be concerned about your privacy. A curtain or private room should be available for a genital exam. If you have a history of trauma, you can request a chaperone during your exam. Never hesitate to ask for what you need to feel comfortable during your physical exam.

About Your Medical Provider

Your care may be provided by a variety of people with varying titles other than your doctor. They have all been trained to evaluate you and work up your concerns. They work together as a team. Regardless of the title of your provider, if you have concerns regarding the type of care you are receiving, you have every right to speak up. Ask for another opinion and we will discuss later how to escalate your care, so you feel safe.

Differential Diagnosis

A differential diagnosis is when your medical provider comes up with a list of the worst that could go on with you. The type of diagnosis that is so severe that if we don't catch it, it could kill you. Providers list these from rare to typical. Rare ones are called zebras for a reason—they aren't common. Your provider must weigh a lot of things when working you up, the risk of performing certain labs or scans on you and your baby. He or she must rule out certain conditions.

Your doctor should discuss with you and help you understand, as best they can, the worst-case scenario. What can wait to be checked by your regular doctor? What must be checked now? We call this shared management decision making. It puts you at the center. It improves your patient experience and satisfaction. It makes your provider an equal, not a dictator, for your care. Tests are ordered to further understand your issue. After the results are in place, your provider will plan the next step.

You should ask yourself if you feel better after care. Did you receive fluids? Pain medication? Nausea medicine?

If you don't feel better, say that you don't.

Together, you and your provider decide if it is safe for you to go home. Do you need follow-up? Further observation? Hospital admittance? Share any concerns and ensure you are fine with the final plans. You can always voice to your provider what you feel.

After seeing you, your provider will document your visit using the framework I shared. Your rights as a patient are to have access to your records, including the notes that are made during your care. Understand that if there are ever any concerns about your care, these records are available to you.

Your Clinician's Role

Throughout history and to this very day, health care hierarchy gives the highest level of power to the doctor. Or, to the surgeon. This means most health care organizations consider the doctor or surgeon as the person who knows it all and can't make diagnosis mistakes.

It's time to change this perception.

I want you to see your provider as a wise monk. They received good training, but they also need you and your story in order to do their job well. So, when tackling and trying to care for you, picture yourself sitting on a bench, working with your doctor or health care provider to solve your health concerns. Do not place the white-coated provider on a pedestal to tell you what to do.

They need you. You need them.

The relationship must be one built on mutual respect and dignity, so you can set clear boundaries from the beginning. Make sure old patterns of the role of your provider aren't affecting your ability to state, question, and challenge all aspects of your care.

Medical providers are human beings. They are not "above" you. No hospital staffer works alone. Your success is their success. Everyone must collaborate and do their part. Seeing them as human tells you they can make mistakes. We need to rely on excellent systems and not only their power or education to prevent errors.

LET'S TALK ABOUT BROKEN TRUST

The hospital can be an unfamiliar place. Some of you have never had a reason to go to an emergency room. Some of you have never been at all because you lack medical insurance. It is understandable, based on stories and experiences you may have heard from family and friends, to have low trust and confidence when you walk through those doors.

That lack of trust can show and transfer when you present for care.

If you have or your family member has had a poor experience before, know that it is a big deal. In some ways, the trauma becomes pain you must heal from. Never hesitate to reach out to a counselor, therapist, or coach if you have been discriminated against. Or, if you have been the victim of bias or severe complications in health care or any part of your life.

You deserve to be seen and heard. You must process trauma so that it doesn't continue to affect your future care. Research shows that a history of racism and discrimination can increase your risk for chronic conditions and complications like pre-eclampsia, so it is important to feel safe and supported.

Never ignore these feelings. Ask yourself, "Why am I upset? Do I need someone else to support me? Do I need family or a patient advocate here? Do I need to start at the top again and present more calmly so I can share why I am here?"

Navigating Communication Breakdowns

"Each time a woman stands up for herself, without knowing it possibly, without claiming it, she stands up for all women."
—Maya Angelou

Our health care system is flawed.

Mama, you will get lost in the shuffle if you don't prepare for transitions or if you lack support.

Continual stressors can overwhelm you while pregnant. Even after childbirth, add in postpartum depression and the role that can play in your recovery, and complications continue.

Communication can be your saving grace.

Miscommunication Traps

During a pandemic or emergency, women can find themselves alone in a clinic or hospital room. This can compound feelings of isolation and feelings of powerlessness that can lead to moms to be, not feeling like they can voice their issues or concerns.

The healthcare team that surrounds you can be impacted by several things. Shift time. Resources. General busyness. Visiting a hospital during the evening or during a shift change can differ from a late-night visit or holiday visit. Also, consider that the hospital may be inadequately staffed for the volume of patients, or there may be an inability to discharge existing patients.

Understanding all these issues can help you understand and expect that medical staffers face issues that affect their ability to hear you clearly.

Many of these events are systemic. While not typically done on purpose, the events can kick off a domino effect—one event happens right after the other, causing a chain reaction. Combine all of this with stress, staff shortages, insufficient specialist resources, and eagerness of the provider to end their shift and go home to family, and you can see how this system creates the perfect storm.

How does this lead to a mama of color not being heard?

How does this impact her issues not being addressed?

I don't know all the answers, as every scenario is specific. However, in my experience as a healthcare provider and also as a mom, I can understand how these scenarios can lead to these perfect storms. Combine that with the different bias or personalities of the medical team and you begin to see a pattern.

Be Aware of the "Side With Me" Phenomenon

I call it the 'side with me' phenomenon.

When you ask for support in a hospital, some staff may be triggered to sway the support team to see their side, or label you as being unreasonable. This is human nature. No one wants to be wrong. Address this head on by stating that you need this person to listen to your issues with a rational mind and not prioritize what may have been said about you.

Tell your story. Tell where the communication went wrong and state what you need to feel cared for? Additional tests? A second opinion? Pain medication? The person is more equipped to work with you and help you communicate exactly what it is you need to the team you are having issues with.

VARIED INTERACTIONS

As a frontline leader, educator, and a clinician, and through my experiences as a patient, I hold a unique perspective. I am intrigued with our healthcare system and how we communicate as teams. I wondered why some teams do such amazing work. And others… well, that's why there is a lot of work to do.

But like me I'm sure you too especially if you have heard horror stories or you yourself have experienced situations where you are wondering why? Did that happen to me? Why were they rude to me? Did she just snap at me? Why did he call security? Situations can escalate quickly, and there are a few things I have observed that lead to this.

DIFFERENT PERSONALITIES

Personalities are so vast. A medical facility is a mixed pot of different cultures and beliefs all thrown together under a common vision, which is do no harm and save lives. Everyone on their first day believes this. However, over time, certain factors affect this. How people belong or fit into their teams. How much do their leaders respect them or treat them well? Are they given the freedom to be creative or is everything spelled out? Do they feel boxed in?

NO COACHING OR LITTLE COACHING

We receive a lot of training in healthcare, but most of it centers on medical knowledge. Some institutions now realize we also need to teach and coach people on how to interact with other people. How to talk on the phone. How to manage emotions. How to state differences in a non-biased way. This is new and of course it takes time to standardize anything in healthcare.

Gatekeeping and Hierarchical Systems

We are supposed to function as a team. However, over the history of medicine much stock has been placed on power levels. This can be the source of communication breakdown—power between doctors, providers, staff, and administration. Currently, the medical world is focused on improving this antiquated dynamic because it causes people to either be afraid to speak up, or to abuse their power.

However, once again, change does not happen quickly.

So how can you be aware and hopefully avoid falling victim to hierarchical dynamics?

Team up with your support squad if you feel you are being overpowered. There is power in numbers.

Talk openly to the provider and ask how they work as a team. Especially if you are getting a high-risk procedure. Is it safe for everyone to voice concerns on the team? Is a simple question you can ask.

In the future, I hope all hospitals enable their teams especially frontline to not be gatekeepers but to use an algorithm when they catch themselves doing so and to facilitate truly centering the needs of the patient.

New Policies

When you think of all the moving parts of a hospital, policies, guidelines, and parameters are so helpful to standardize how we deal with common issues. So, policies can be effective, now how each individual implements these policies is a whole different matter. It can be used as armor. Defended to the death. And we are not thinking that policies are supposed to be evaluated routinely especially in events where they don't work to serve or protect the patient.

COVID-19 brought a rapid onslaught of policies that were made in haste to keep patients safe and staff safe however sometimes they caused inadvertently extreme suffering to some individuals...and this is where our healthcare systems fail us instead of viewing policies as fluid and creating opportunities for discussion when they cause suffering to the people, they are supposed to protect they can do more harm than the good they intended to.

When my twins were in the NICU, I knew based on my research that the one thing that would bring them home faster was to give them as much interaction and holding as much as possible. With twins that meant I was there for 11-12 hour stretches. When I was still in the hospital recovering, the policy stated I could touch both of them and spend as much time as possible. However, right after my discharge, when I started daily NICU visits, the very first visit my husband and I were met by a nurse who immediately put her hand up and said only one of you can be here at a time. Just one parent.

We looked at one another and said, "But we have twins?"

They quickly spat out the rest of the policy. "You cannot see both babies on the same day. Only one each day."

We were puzzled. I burst into tears. We had smashed against a policy created out of fear that was supposed to keep me and my babies safe from COVID, instead it caused suffering. I had to choose which baby to see. Even worse, it could affect how quickly the babies grew and how fast I could take them home.

The other parents fell in line. My husband and I saw babies only being able to be seen for short periods of time. I wondered if they had read the same articles about skin to skin contact and knew how it could help their babies in countless ways.

My husband and I devised a system to account for this. We did two shifts. He took the morning shift, and I took the evening shift. We would FaceTime as much as possible.

I always wonder how I would have approached that experience as a healthcare leader, especially being on the receiving end as a patient. If I encountered that policy today, I would have involved a social worker in the process because most hospitals have them, and they are more skilled on how to communicate with different backgrounds and counsel through difficult times. I couldn't think of a better time especially being deep into my postpartum blues and going through what was a traumatic experience on top of the already traumatizing event of your children being in the hospital. I would have done telephone consults post discharge to discuss the new policy and create opportunities to have frequent feedback since it was new. We could have come up with alternate decisions or review of the policies, such as exceptions for parents of multiples using personal protective equipment (PPE). Because the same nurse who also came from the outside daily could touch and interact with my babies, yet I wasn't. Policies can be made without considering all scenarios, so they need to be fluid.

What can you do when a policy is causing you distress? Escalate! Escalate! Escalate!

Every day I asked to speak to the directors. Unfortunately, managers and charge nurses and supervisors are typically gate keepers as well. Yes, they can be involved in policymaking, but directors are better positioned to escalate concern that can effect change.

During my issue with seeing my twins, we spoke with the director as often as possible, calmly explaining our distress and helping him see it. He sympathized. It wasn't a quick change, it never is, but in a few months the rules changed. Parents of multiples could hold both their babies.

Here is what you can do:
- If a director is not willing to speak, ask for a social worker.
- Ask for a patient advocate.
- Ask for an incident report which will force leaders to evaluate the problem and look at it from a different perspective.

STRESSED SITUATIONS AND LOW STAFF

It is common that hospitals are more staffed from Monday to Friday, from nine to five. Hospitals often struggle to keep a strong staff on evenings, weekends and holidays, and are typically skeleton during these times. These are the times that lead to breakdown and bad care. I have seen and experienced this time and time again—residents trying to convince doctors they have a serious case, with nurses running haggard covering high patient workloads.

PERSONAL BIAS/RACISM/CONFIRMATION BIAS

When you walk in the doors of a hospital, I cannot predict where you as a mama and especially a minority mother may encounter an adverse event or issue. However, it is important to remember that when you walk through those doors everyone is not against you. The leadership is not conspiring against you. This is the story you may tell yourself when you encounter, disrespect, rudeness, and so on. It is usually limited to that individual and whatever stress they may be dealing with, whether personal or from the work environment. Remember to isolate it to that person. Don't tolerate it. But don't take your anger or frustration to the next person you encounter, especially your provider. This will affect your ability to convey what brought you in the first place in a clear manner and be heard.

If the front desk staff who checked on you greeted you with a snarl, and rudely asks you to sit over there, disarm immediately. Be empathetic when you talk. Try saying, "Is everything OK with you today? I know it can be tough when it's busy, but you spoke to me in a rude manner and that didn't make me feel welcome."

Then, be silent allow for a response. No matter how uncomfortable it is.

If the answer you get is inappropriate and defensive, take a

note. You can ask for their name calmly if it warrants that.
Remember to provide feedback later.

Let it go. Do not assume.

However, never tolerate a lack of respect.

I promise you it is not what any hospital stands for and there
is not a leader on the planet that should ever tolerate it. You can
casually bring it up to your next staff interaction—preferably
with your provider. Name the person. Label the behavior (rude,
cursing, eye-rolling, and so on). Detail your encounter with the
person and state the person's name. Mention that you hope all is
well, but you will provide feedback after the appointment.
Afterward, drop it and focus on the main reason you are there.

TRIAGE RESPONSIBILITY MISMATCH

Rigid policies can sometimes paralyze well intended healthcare
workers because it has been ingrained in them that X, Y, or Z can
happen if this happens. They get buttonholed to that being the
only way to achieve patient safety or adhere to the goals set by
the institution. In a high-stress situation, the person cannot think
creatively.

I'll give you an example. One time a pregnant friend of mine
was listed on the wait list to be induced due to low fluid levels.
This was an extremely stressful moment for her. She was aware
of the risk, but the staff did not stratify and instead placed her on
the list with every other person waiting to be induced.
Technically, medical providers lack a measure for this. And, if
triaged appropriately, she should have been at the top of the list.

But the worker doing their job said, "There is a list we have
been told XYZ, if you have an emergency go to the ER."

However, my friend may never have known if there was an
emergency. When she called me, she was given advice that she
had to advocate for herself and say I wouldn't know if there is
something wrong. Please don't put me on the list with others, as
my doctor was concerned. I also asked her to have her doctor do

the same and call and share how she wasn't a typical patient waiting to be induced.

In high-stress situations such as low staffing, it's hard to be creative and only focus on the rules that have been set. On a Twitter feed I came across, I once read about a baby needing to be transferred to a higher level of care, but they were out of identification bands. The staff called a 'code stork' and made the baby wait an hour instead of escalating immediately to a downtime band that was handwritten so that no harm comes to the patient when trying to follow a policy rigid, which makes sense on its own, but not when a patient's safety is at risk.

Speaking Up at the Hospital

"Our lives begin to end the day we become silent about things that matter."

—Dr. Martin Luther King, Jr.

Sadly, some medical providers may hold conscious (or subconscious) opinions about who they believe deserves help. As a result, they might dismiss a request for medical attention based on insignificant things such as look or appearance. This type of bias, racism, and marginalization can cause you to distrust your provider, make you second guess how you feel, and doubt that you need attention for your body or your baby.

The bottom line? If you feel bad, find medical help. Trust your instincts and seek the support you need to avoid a negative health outcome. Sometimes women who sidestep getting help end up rushing to the hospital later, crashing, and very sick.

Mama, I understand. If you can't trust your provider, it is extremely hard to let them help you. However, you must do your best to communicate early and talk clearly about your issues.

Here are the top ten things to do when you arrive at the medical facility:

Write Down Your Symptoms

As soon as you reach the emergency room or clinic, after the intake person asks you to wait, clearly jot down your feelings and symptoms. Or if you are too weak or in pain to write, think through your symptoms.

Headache. Blurred vision. Dizziness. Nausea. Abdominal cramps. Bleeding. Shoulder pain. No matter what it is, detail every symptom that made you leave your world to find help. Be as specific as possible. Make a list from most severe to least severe — but make sure you share it all. The fast pace of a hospital can be overwhelming, and you may forget to share something important.

Detail the duration of your symptoms. How long have you been feeling this way? Did your symptoms come and go? Have they happened before?

Ask For an Interpreter If Needed

Ask for an interpreter if English is not your first language and you are having trouble communicating your issue. Avoid using slang.

Most MDs and medical providers are classically trained, and they will listen for certain keywords when you speak. Words like pain, bleeding, trouble *breathing*, and so on, will trigger their thinking and guide the path they will use as they work with you. Beating around the bush or sharing distracting information can mislead your care. Again, write it down if you can.

Depending on the setting, for example, an emergency room, the most serious concerns are the ones that will be addressed. The doctor in charge may also have you follow up with your regular provider for less urgent concerns, so be sure you have been clear about the concerns that alarm you, and that you are clear about the issues that can wait.

REMEMBER YOUR HISTORY

Your health history is very important. It puts the provider on the right path of care for you. Only you can clearly state what's bothering you. Your provider needs this information. Without it, you may leave without the right level of medical attention. Your doctor must work with you to ensure your needs have been addressed.

Ask your medical provider, "I came in for this on XXX day. It concerned me. Have we done what we need to check that could be emergent if not addressed? Can you share what those issues are? What does follow-up look like?"

PREPARE KEY INFORMATION

You should prepare key health information **ahead of time**. Your physical history is helpful information for your medical provider. When you are sick, you might not feel like answering a thousand questions. Many of us have amazing relationships with our obstetrician (OB) but we may have to visit a specialist or go to the emergency room. Be prepared for these visits with information to give to a medical provider.

SPEAK CALMLY

Frustration and anger may affect how you are heard. Meditate. Take a deep breath. After waiting for three hours in a waiting room, and possibly encountering rudeness from the intake team, by the time you see a medical professional, your patience may be worn thin. You may be emotionally charged as you try to discuss your issues. This could affect the receptiveness of the provider.

Activate Your Support Squad

Plan to activate your support squad early. In a pandemic or endemic setting, you may be alone for most or all of your care. While you are waiting, text or call someone from your support squad to share what's going on. Ask them to be on standby. Your spouse. A friend. A sister. Anyone trustworthy who has your best interest at heart. It is really helpful if you have a friend with a medical background who understands how hospitals and clinics operate. Support can also be that person remaining on the phone as a witness to listen to the discussions between you and your provider.

Trust Your Hospital Team

Trust that the team in the hospital is ultimately there to care for you. However, they may be under pressures that are not visible to you.

Demand their attention! If you feel less is being done than you require, ask the provider, "What is urgent that should be checked? What needs to be done right now? What can wait to be assessed later?"

Activate Your Hospital Team

Activate your hospital team if needed: patient advocate, social worker, charge nurse, etc. Calmly say, "I'm not feeling heard because of XYZ…"

Ask for a re-explanation if you don't understand something. Never assume if you are confused. Ask for a simpler answer.

Never tolerate rude or inappropriate behavior. The hospital does not tolerate it either, so use your hospital team to handle it. Don't do it yourself or be combative.

Follow Your Medical Provider's Advice

If you need to follow up, please do so. Don't delay. I know life gets busy, but your actions could save your life. So, follow up when recommended and set that appointment immediately. Being lost to follow up is a dangerous thing that can lead to a bad outcome. The earlier a problem can be caught the better.

Give feedback on the care you received—hospitals care about the patient experience, and that includes yours. Don't keep your experience to yourself, especially if it was bad. Take names of your care team, and if care was inadequate, provide that feedback. No one is perfect. Our health care system isn't perfect either. That is why it is important they learn from the mistakes. But rarely do patients give feedback regarding poor experiences or outcomes.

Seek a Second Opinion

Never be afraid to seek a second opinion if you feel it is warranted. I know additional healthcare is not always affordable, but if your clinician says something can wait based on a phone conversation and you feel it worsening, don't wait. The ego or feelings of your provider or health care team is never above yours.

Visit the ER to be checked out. Remember, your condition can worsen. If your picture of health changes don't follow the old recommendations for a worsening issue. Pride and ego are unimportant. Your provider would rather you be safe than sorry. So, if you talked at 3:00 PM and your symptoms weren't as bad, and they said over the phone you can wait to be seen the next few days. However, if the problem has worsened (for example, bleeding or spotting) at 2:00 AM, and you have a bad feeling about it, trust yourself. Since your clinician cannot see the new picture, seek urgent/emergent care immediately. In these

situations, don't be afraid to abandon previous advice —
remember, those directives were based on how you felt earlier,
not now. Your story is the most important part. You are
ultimately in charge of your care.

After you are given instructions, ask yourself, "Do I
understand what my doctor, healthcare provider or nurse...just
said, really?" Stop and listen. Providers often state the same
advice daily. They can speak fast and summarize. They don't
always make sure you understand what has been said.
Sometimes you shake your head because you may not want to
admit you didn't understand. So, for information especially
regarding risk and what to do if something goes wrong, please
teach your doctor what was said to you so they can be sure you
understood. This is called the teach back method. It is used often
but not always, so get used to using it. Take notes and repeat
what was said to make sure you understood.

A second opinion is nothing more than you needing more
data to make a more informed decision especially when the
stakes could not be higher, your health and that of your baby.
Here are additional reasons you may want to seek a second
opinion:

- Your provider incorrectly says something is a 100%
  certain or uncertain without a full spectrum of test
  results. Or the provider changes the information
  regarding the prognosis or outcome for your
  diagnosis, and you are confused and unsure despite
  trying to get clarification. Nothing is ever a 100%
  certain in medicine there is always room for hope and
  uncertainty.
- Your provider asks you to make a non-reversible
  decision in a rushed manner, before waiting for test
  results to return, or getting a full picture in a non-
  urgent setting.

I'll give you an example. A dear mama once shared that the provider at her 13-week ultrasound, before awaiting further testing or asking for a diagnostic ultrasound from a specialist, told her to abort the baby and that the baby had zero chance of survival. It turned out the radiologist had read the ultrasound wrong. Thankfully, results of the genetic testing ordered came back after the mama had already made several out of state calls to terminate her pregnancy. Had she lived in a state where she could terminate her child easily, the child would no longer exist. The genetic testing results concluded no findings of a pregnancy that would not survive. She used the phrase 'zero percent chance of survival'. Yikes!

Fortunately, this mama picked up the phone when she read the test that was in her mail. That was when the doctor said that maybe it was not a zero chance as she had thought.

This dear mama then bravely asked for a second opinion from a specialist she had to travel six hours to see. The specialist said, "Why are you here? You and your baby are healthy." He saw no such issues and that her baby was as healthy as could be. She was relieved but also distraught as she had already started calling clinics outside her state to terminate her pregnancy.

Pay attention. Before any finite and irreversible decisions are made, ensure testing has occurred and understand you have a right to a second opinion.

Final Reminders

Last, remember why you visited the hospital. Review your symptoms. The human mind is amazing. You can minimize anything even serious issues/symptoms.

Also, when you have waited for hours to be seen, you may feel better. It can be hard for medical staff to prioritize someone who appears well in an ER or is not doubled over in pain, especially on a busy short-staffed night. For example, during a pandemic when you have been waiting for hours. Let's say you feel better and tell yourself, "I'll just wait. I have crying kids at home. I will come back tomorrow or call my clinic doctor."

Or, even as you are being seen, you may sense the staff giving you *'you came to the ER for this'* look as they check your vitals. Your vitals may show no immediate warning signs or may have improved while you waited. Doubt can creep in. This is a dangerous point. If you don't clearly share the issues that made you drive for an hour at 2:00 AM and leave your three or four kids at home, you might leave. Combine that with an overworked tired hospital staff who may not take the time to break down or define your issue.

Your doctor's ability to think through this can save your life. In the ER, you want your doctor to rule out issues this can save your life. Don't go home until all your issues are addressed. Talk about this with your medical team. Tell them what made you come in and leave your family time and ask them to rule serious issues out (for example, pre-eclampsia) before you leave.

As a minority woman, it can be incorrectly assumed that you may bear or have more pain tolerance because you look well instead of agitated. As though your issues can be delayed to a later date when more staff is available. Watch out for this! We must dispel this assumption that minority women feel less pain. Pain is pain. State that though you look fine, you *do not feel fine*. You need to be checked. Repeat your issues as many times as needed. Activate your squad electronically if you don't feel heard and are breaking down.

You always have the right to say no or refuse care. This is your body. You are in full control. All decisions made should be agreed upon unless lifesaving and you are not able to. If you don't agree with medication, tests, or imaging ordered for you, speak clearly about your concerns. You can always say no. However, when you refuse care or demand to leave you may need to sign an AMA-against medical advice form. So, voice your concerns. Is there a substitute for the recommended care? You can also ask for a second opinion from another provider in the same facility in some cases.

Never Ignore These Symptoms

"Tune in to your body, mind, and soul and heed their warnings."
—Oprah Winfrey

As a new clinician, my head was in the clouds regarding what I needed to watch for during and after having my twins. As new moms, we are so busy, and I know that our appointments with our providers are quick. What I learned that was surprising is that we need to know that we are at risk one year after delivery for some conditions.

Time to review the symptoms you should always know and must escalate as needed. These symptoms should be considered seriously before and after you have had your baby!

The window to be vigilant is up to year after the pregnancy, so continue to be mindful of your health and body by getting your follow-up appointments and bringing any concerns to the attention of your provider. Share these signs with your support squad, partner family so that they can also help you recognize these signs early as well and support you.

When you present to a hospital ER with symptoms, don't wait in line! Walk over and share your symptoms. Tell the staff you are pregnant or have just been pregnant.

SEVERE SWELLING

Arms. Legs. Hands. Feet. Pregnancy can naturally bring about swelling to your body. However, swelling to your hands and face can be a sign of pre-eclampsia. This issue must be evaluated fast. Pre-eclampsia can occur after delivery, especially within six weeks after pregnancy.

If you have severe swelling, don't wait in line. Rush to the front desk and let them know you are pregnant or just had a baby. Also, if there is swelling in your legs with pain and/or redness seek immediate evaluation.

SHORTNESS OF BREATH OR TROUBLE BREATHING

During pregnancy, this may be hard to differentiate from late trimester shortness of breath, so be mindful of changes especially if worsening. Notice if you cannot get enough air or if you are having chest pain or tightness. Seek immediate help if you feel something is wrong. If you have a pulse oximeter to check your oxygen levels at home, this could guide you, and if you have levels that are below your baseline you have established with your provider seek help as soon as possible.

HEADACHE

A headache can also be hard to differentiate, especially for those with history of migraines. If you have the following characteristics of a headache, seek help!

Does the headache start suddenly? Include blurred vision? Do you see spots? Are you nauseous or dizzy? Does the headache continue even after medication or hydration? This can be a sign of pre-eclampsia. Seek care immediately, especially if you also have elevated blood pressure and/or lower and upper extremity swelling.

Vaginal Bleeding or Discharge

During pregnancy, talk about bleeding with your health care provider. Seek immediate care if you are bleeding heavily, soaking a pad hourly, or passing clots. Also, foul smelling vaginal discharge should be evaluated.

Additional Symptoms Requiring Immediate Attention

- Abdominal pain
- Chest pain
- Fever temperature over 101 or 100.4
- Dizziness or fainting episodes
- Elevated, slowed, or irregular heartbeat
- Vision changes
- Mental state changes (can't talk or think clearly or having thoughts of harm to yourself or others)

Other Body Issues

Remember that your body can still get sick while pregnant. Perform your breast exams regularly. If you feel anything, do not assume a lump or strange swelling is because of pregnancy. One in 3000 women will develop breast cancer. Get any lumps checked out.

Early Pregnancy Symptoms to Check

- Abdominal pain cramping
- Vaginal bleeding

Later Pregnancy (greater than 20 weeks) Symptoms to Check

- Change in vision
- Itchy skin, hand, feet
- Swelling to legs hands, face
- Baby not moving as much or stopped moving
- Severe headache
- Dizziness, fainting
- Shortness of breath
- Fast or slow heart rate
- Pain in your side or beneath your ribcage that does not go away

Pregnancy Symptoms to Check at Any Time

- Fever or chills
- Frequent urination with burning or pain
- Vaginal discharge that is foul smelling
- Vaginal bleeding
- Trauma to your belly (fall, accident, or due to domestic violence)
- Dizziness, fainting
- Shortness of breath
- Fast or slow heart rate
- Feelings of depression, anxiety, self-harm, or other thoughts affecting your daily tasks.
- Headaches
- Chest pain
- Abdominal pain

Post Pregnancy - Six Weeks to a Year

- Fever temperature more than 101 or 100.4
- Dizziness or fainting episodes
- Frequent urination with burning or pain
- Vaginal discharge that is foul smelling
- Vaginal bleeding
- Elevated, slowed, or irregular heartbeat
- Change in vision
- Change in mental state (can't talk or think clearly or thoughts of harm to yourself or others)
- Headaches
- Chest pain
- Abdominal pain

Setting Up Support, Self-Care, and Prevention

"When women are healthy and supported, they can do anything."

—Christy Turlington

MAMA, besides a birth plan, you will need a support plan after having baby. Your support plan is a one-year strategy for help and support as you heal, and your baby adjusts to life in the world.

ANECDOTE

One of the main reasons I wrote this book was that when I read or listened to the news, maternal hope seemed nonexistent. Every story or statistic was riddled with horrific situations that troubled me and made me fearful of pregnancy. What could I do to gain hope? I wasn't sure.

I want you to have a different experience.

I want you to know there is hope. Help is on the way, and you can do a lot to help yourself and others. Certainly, awareness can help, and you'll notice things you can do through reading books like this one. But I want to turn your attention to one other tremendous tool in your toolkit: support.

Support is a forgotten word we just don't use enough. It should be prescribed because it is the biggest protective buffer, we have to decrease the stress and sometimes the distress associated with pregnancy. Research points to this and it should not be left up to the mama to figure out all on her own after pregnancy. We need to plan now, again don't just make a birth plan make a postpartum support plan for a year after birth, those are the most vulnerable times for all mothers, and I hope that if you take anything away from this guide this will be the way you think about support, not as optional or a nice to have, but a must-have and literally a life saver and good indicator for the health of you and your baby, so not having it or setting it up could cost you.

The predominant word I hear is **self-care**. Self-care for a pregnant woman is like Greek. A vague term thrown around. When I first heard it, I thought it meant I should leave my twins at home to go out for a pedicure or go shopping and that I would feel better. But I didn't. Self-care is a terrible word to throw at a birthing person during pregnancy; we need to realize that there is no self in the insurmountable task that a mother bringing a baby has to go through in the world. I think there is a more important word that should be taught to any woman considering having children. It is a word assumed to be available to every birthing person but is actually not.

That word is SUPPORT.

My mind was blown when I reviewed the research, which showed that low support during pregnancy not just affected emotional wellbeing but physical and in a big way. Low support can increase stress, which can increase risk for substance abuse, mental illness, and poor health outcomes. Lack of support can also elevate your risk for complications such as hypertensive disorders, and so on.

In the future, I want every birthing person to assess their own support status, and hopefully every maternal provider, doula, and coach to assess this and work together in the pregnancy, with every birthing person. Just like staying healthy and eating and moving well is recommended, we also need to build supports up. This is lifesaving. More lifesaving than self-care. In fact, it is the precursor to self-care. Without support, self-care feels like an insurmountable task. Sometimes, it may be uncomfortable or impossible. Self-care goes hand in hand with support. It is the byproduct of support.

What does support mean? You may think having a partner, a mother or mother-in-law is all you need. Why is that not enough? You must thoroughly assess your support. Do you have a committed partner, mother, mother-in-law, or grandmother, father, father-in-law, or grandfather? Do you have support that is truly available or do they work a lot? Is your partner and family emotionally unavailable? Do they have a history of mental illness? Substance abuse? Do they want to support you, do they know how to support you?

Even if you are surrounded by many friends and family members, they may not know how to support you. As a birthing person, you must learn to ask for the support you need. Also, if you don't have a partner, biological mother, or surrogate mother to play that role, you may unknowingly experience low support. If this is the case, you should definitely ask for support. Many mothers will provide that support without being asked. Also know that your support team does not need to look a certain way, or be of a certain gender. They only need to be people that have you and your babies' best interests and are willing to help as they can. Don't expect certain people to provide certain help, ask for what you need and prepare for an honest response.

Don't give up. Get creative and ask people. Think about friends, extended family members, your faith or spiritual support groups, neighbors and more.

Support Types

What is support? Is it all the same? According to the research, every type of support is not the same. Certain types of support can be more valuable than others. In literature I have read, there are three types: tangible, affectionate support, and emotional/information support (positivity, advice, and empathy).

So which type, when you lack it, causes the most stress and anxiety? You guessed it... affectionate support. What does this mean? I know some of us our romantic relationships can be in peril before, during, and after pregnancy, and our partner or spouse may not offer us this support. The source does not have to be romantic, a hug can go a long way during postpartum from anyone in your support team.

What If I Am an Unmothered Mother?

I spent a lot of my childhood observing the relationship of mothers and daughters. My grandmother and her mother. My father and his mother. My stepmom and her mother. My friends and their mothers. They were all unique, beautiful, and special in their way. They all possessed a common theme of unconditional love. They would all drop what they were doing in a moment's notice for one another. Now I'm not naïve enough to think that all mother-child relationships are rosy. Some are absent due to whatever ills plague them (for example, because of substance abuse or mental illness).

But I'm still curious of the origin.

Was it because of poor relationships with their own mothers? Low support that didn't give them the dots to connect for a healthy mother child relationship? As a mother, I think of this more and more. I've dedicated my life to becoming self-aware either from therapy or coaching. I know relationships can be harder for me because of this gap—particularly trusting relationships.

What does this mean to you, dear unmothered mama?

Well, having a child requires high levels of social support to weather the storms that may come your way. If the support is not readily available for you in the form of your own mother, you must seek it where you can. You will need a mom squad, you need to learn to allow them to mother you, and it may never come close to filling the gap left by not having your own nurturing and dedicated mother especially if you once knew her, but you will always need that nurturing wherever you can get it. Surrogate mothers. Aunts. Stepmothers. Sisters. Cousins. Friends. You name it. Know that you may start from a place where you may not be as natural at understanding this precious bond. It might be harder for you to receive this type of support because you are not used to it. Perhaps you've been self-sufficient all your life. Your instinct may be like mine, which was, "I'll be fine' thank you." Put your ego aside for the next couple of years and aggressively build your reliable support system around you. Research shows that you are most at risk for complications if with no support.

SUPPORT FOR RETURNING TO WORK

The role colleagues and co-workers and employers can play are limitless in supporting and helping new mothers prevent and reduce their risks for complications. It is not news that America's programs for maternity leave are the worst amongst other developed countries. It is important to acknowledge the role that may be playing in the mortality of mothers especially with maternity leave time hovering under three months, which is all too common in our country. As well as the lack of mandatory paid leave for all mothers? Especially single mothers and those with financial instability, which leads patients to go back to work in as little as two weeks. Remember the information shared earlier on the healing going on in the body, the risk of postpartum depression which affects over 20% of moms, the stress of working so soon after childbirth in my opinion can contribute to maternal mortality, not being able to make follow up appointments, chronic stress, inability to nurture or even breast feed appropriately if chosen. Sadly, research shows that minorities especially black women tend to be more affected with low access to jobs with supportive or any paid leave and may account for the disparities in outcomes.

We must stop underestimating the effect of stress during and after pregnancy on our mothers, there is no greater stress on a mother than going back to work in the final weeks of the third trimester and so quickly after pregnancy and the tears and pain I have heard other moms express is something we must continue to fight to undo. Employers must continue to review and improve polices on paid leave for moms towards the end of pregnancy and postpartum. Our government must enact and pass laws that provide meaningful paid maternity leave for all mothers. Balancing the cost of childcare with low support and returning to work is a recipe for disastrous outcomes that so many women endure.

A DAILY WELL ROUTINE

Develop a morning routine. Run, walk, or journal. Stretch, do yoga, or dance to your favorite song. You can do this for as little as 5-10 minutes per day and it will make a big difference in how you feel physically. As I shared earlier self-care can feel like calculus for some in the early postpartum, a checklist for mom can help to check off if she has done certain things each day, like sleep at least 4-5 hours, shower, eat a nutritious meal, take a walk, family and your support squad can help with accountability for the checklist especially those that may be experiencing the postpartum blues or depression.

Consider Hiring a Doula

Get a doula at any point in your pregnancy. It is never too late. I am not a doula, but I advocate the job of doulas and I advocate using one. To this day I regret not having one while pregnant with my twins. It was the best thing I could have done.

Medical providers and doulas must work together to provide the highest level of care. They both have different roles to play in the eco-system that is pregnancy.

Have a Creative Outlet

A creative outlet is important. Even if you are busy, grieving, or overwhelmed, you are still a person. You don't have to spend every moment being a mom. Singing. Dancing. Painting. Creating a custom garden. Any of these activities can help ease stress in your life. Think outside the box here, anytime you can spend creating, building and designing something that is authentic to you gives an amazing opportunity to rest creatively.

Self-Love

We need to be close to others. Men are better than us at self-care. Social isolation is hazardous to our health, increases risk of death than smoking and obesity.

Complete a Hospital Tour

During the height of the pandemic, many women could not go on hospital tours. While having my twins, I was sad I didn't get to do this, but I realize now that I didn't really know the right things to care about on that tour. I was more concerned about my babies. Where would they stay? How would they be kept safe so no one steals them? In my experiences, I had seen a few 'baby stork' activities (where a baby had been taken from the unit). So, all I cared about was reviewing how the hospital tagged babies appropriately to prevent switches.

When you are ready to go on your local area hospital tours, and I highly recommend that you do, be sure to understand based on your risk factors of your health and pregnancy, low, mod, or high risk that the facility you have picked can support you as well as baby.

If your doctor says you are high risk, you should go to the right hospital with the infrastructure to care for your condition. According to research, this one act increases your chance of survival and going to the wrong hospital could be the difference between life or death.

During your hospital tour reconcile what the hospital can provide you in terms of your care when something does go wrong because it can, though rare but especially if you know you are high risk, be aware for you and for baby. Talk about it with your provider so you can plan options and know where you can go for the best care for you.

Ask your OB-GYN where they have privileges (rights to practice) so that they can take care of you if they are available.

Next where will you go if you have an emergency? Preferably somewhere that can take care of both you and baby. See below the different classifications of hospitals and their ability to support you and baby.

I know geographically you may not have an option where you choose to get care, but it is helpful to understand what services are available in the hospital you will access care. Ask questions of your provider and hospital. Promote open communication. Stay aware of practices and policies that may affect or impact your delivery and postpartum stay.

Most of us assume every hospital can do the same thing based on things like their size or name. But this is not the case. Certain branches, especially those in rural areas, may not have full capacity or access to specialists and may have to call those services in during specific windows or they may have to transfer you for higher levels of care. It's best to know this beforehand so you can decide with your family and provider a plan in the event these situations occur.

MATERNAL HEALTH HOSPITAL LEVELS AND DESIGNATIONS

If unable to go on a tour, visit the hospital website. Or even better, call to confirm the level of care the hospital provides to both you and baby so you can make an informed decision.

Lower levels and levels 3 and 4 are expected to have collaborations to ensure safe transport of patients for higher level of care when needed as well as continued education for lower levels that may not have experience managing more complex patients. Below you will find designation and definition for each of the level of care for mothers, there are 4 levels and there is also a birthing center. This information may not be readily available, and you have to ask for it. That will change with time. It is easier and more transparent to find out the levels of care for your infant.

During the tour, compare the level of care for you and baby. If you are high-risk, at minimum, both levels of care should be level 3 or 4. Confirm with your provider which is most appropriate and available for you.

Hospital Levels:

- Birthing center - This is a center that cares for low-risk women having single babies that are expected to be uncomplicated births. A birthing center is most likely not capable of performing a C-section. Be sure to ask if the center is accredited, and also ask what care escalation would look like for you.
- Level 1 (basic) - These clinics are not attached to a hospital and may not be able to do a caesarean section. They can be staffed by midwives. They can help women who have uncomplicated twin gestation, those

with stable gestational diabetes, pre-eclampsia with mild symptoms. This clinic should have access to a physician that can do emergency c section at all times, must have a system to transfer to higher level of care when needed.

- Level 2 – A level 2 hospital with C-section capabilities. If the OB can't make it, another doctor or OB nurse can support placenta previa, chronic conditions like diabetes, asthma, and chronic hypertension. Can perform CT scan, MRI, ultrasound, also 24/7 anesthesia, general surgeons, and hospitalist.
- Level 3 - Includes all of Level 2 plus Level 3. Can see moderate cases of heart disease, patients with placenta issues suspected, they have an onsite medical and surgical provided with a critical care ICU to support someone on ventilator, pre-eclampsia, auto immune or liver or bleeding disorders. Hospital has an in-house hospitalist ready if your local OB can't make it in time. Psychiatric care specialist is also available within time frame.
- Level 4 — Includes all of level 3 plus level 4. Caretakers are able to care for very sick patients that have severe heart conditions, may need neurosurgery, heart surgery, are unstable or need organ transplant. Maternal ICU in labor and delivery 24/7 access to specialists.

There are tons of questions I know you will ask on your tour, about the nursery, your room, and other functions. Below are questions to ask on your hospital tour (or by phone):

- Is the hospital or care center level 1, 2, 3, or 4?
- If the hospital is lower level, how is care escalated?

- If a severe complication occurs, are they able to care for you there or will you need to be transferred? How about the babies?
- What is the ratio of nurse to patient…how do they staff during a shortage?
- What happens when the hospital is full? How do you triage who comes in to be delivered? How do I escalate if I need care?
- With whom do I share my birth plan?
- Do you have a list of doulas or midwives?
- In the event I have a concern about my care, who can I call on to help—patient advocate or social worker? Can I have their numbers?

Bonus points once you have decided on your hospital to call and introduce yourself, to discuss how to get support.

If a nurse or staff member is being discourteous, biased, or racist, what is the best way to handle those situations? At the moment, yes, you may feel like a complete zebra and the person giving the hospital tour may look at you like a deer in headlights. You can always say it's okay if you don't know this, but can you see if your manager or director has those answers?

Lastly, ask about the following:

- Pandemic protocols and the hospital visitation policy.
- Can you come and go in the event you are discharged before your child?
- Doulas? Can they participate in my care?
- Midwives are they available?

ASSEMBLING YOUR SUPPORT SQUAD

"You can never have too much love and support from your tribe
— it's the most powerful force in the world."
—Unknown

THE TITLE of this guide is *Save Yourself Mama* because it is time
we stop underestimating how much of a role we can play in our
own health.

I was no stranger to being a patient before having my twin
girls. Through the years, I had undergone several medical visits
and over ten procedures and surgeries, and I felt confident in my
experience as a patient when I visited the ER that day when I
physically felt off about three weeks after my girls were born.

Something was different this time that I had not noticed, and
it was the feeling of loneliness, when my husband dropped me
off at the front doors and we were told no family could join me, I
felt lonely, and these feelings were most likely heightened by
being freshly postpartum and dealing with so much emotionally
especially the consuming thoughts of my daughters in the NICU
fighting for their lives. I remember that walk into the hospital
and the feeling of me against everyone else in the hospital with
no one to support me, where ordinarily pre-pandemic I'd have

had my husband and even a friend or two join me or at least be able to.

In this chapter you will learn about the importance of support, not only general pre- and postpartum for your pregnancy, but a specific plan you must create and a squad you must designate. My fellow BIPOC women and birthing persons should have a squad to activate for any issues that arise when seeking care. In the next section, we will delve deeper into support, but for now let's talk about your health care support squad.

Spend your nine months cultivating a support squad if you lack it. Especially in the three months before baby's birth, actively recruit and ensure commitment from your support squad members. These are people that have accepted that when you find yourself alone, unheard or needing support of any kind in a healthcare setting, they are willing to be on speaker and listen or even go with you to your appointment. You need 3-4 people max on your squad.

If you can afford it, pay for life saving support. This looks like a doula, or maternal health coach, especially for those without available and supportive parents, spouses, and extended families.

Designate your go-to person on the squad. This will be the person you call if you find yourself in a healthcare setting that ignores you. Have a conversation beforehand of the support you may need for them, and no they do not need to have any medical experience, they can just be on the line to listen and reiterate your concerns and support you if you feel like giving up, they can get more support for you if needed.

On a personal note, if I could do it all again, I would have spent more time building a support plan and not just a squad. Especially now being aware of the risk factors that made me susceptible to not being heard and seen. A spouse alone cannot be expected to provide full support, this expectation stresses so many relationships. I couldn't have done it alone. Bless my husband. He did his best, but to this day I regret not making the financial sacrifice to hire a doula, maternal-focused therapist, or social worker to join my squad. I had pre-conceived notions that these were luxury items. I didn't realize they were lifesaving. These individuals can play key roles in reducing mortality. The women I knew who had used services such as a night nurse or a doula all had more disposable income. And so, I assumed they were not a necessity. Playing to my narrative of having to be a strong black woman could have cost me my life. I am a black woman, but I never have to be strong to prove anything to anyone or worse at risk of jeopardizing my health or the health of my family.

Build that support system before you walk in that hospital door!

The concept of a team in healthcare is not new. When you enter those doors, there is a team with members who know each other. They work together to see you, and usher you through your healthcare experience. Health care is collaborative. No one works alone. They need support. Guess what? You are part of that team, and you also need support. The team is supposed to hear your needs. The team takes your concerns seriously and looks into them. If you feel this is not happening, or if you think the health care team members are not doing enough to care for you, activate your support squad immediately. This step can save your life. Even if you are the most knowledgeable person, make sure you have a team going in.

Preparing Your Support Plan and Squad

In the first few weeks you discover you are expecting, take some time to design what support system you may need around you.

This is part one of your support plan. Create this alongside your birth plan. Create your support plan to cover time spanning before baby's birth until up to one year after birth. Set your ego and pride aside as you plan, your tendency to be a lone wolf, again you are increasing the survival for you and baby.

You will need:

- Support for your health care needs
- Support for pregnancy
- Support for work, yes you can include a plan for financial support too.
- Support for postpartum

Create a calendar, use your church community, friends, neighbors or whomever, and use rosters to have people sign up for shifts. Not only to drop food off but to visit and help with any and everything. Laundry. Mail. Groceries. Organizing. Pet care. You name it. It may sound cliche, but this preparation can reduce your risk for postpartum depression and even complications in some situations.

When I think back to the day, I found out I was pregnant and the many lists I made of things I would need, I read countless books and blogs, top ten things I would need to get ready for baby. They were mainly focused on the baby, or at least I mostly focused there. What I truly needed was clear guidance regarding the top ten things I should prepare during and beyond my pregnancy.

Today I realize I never created a support network or actual plan for myself.

According to research, society today veers away from the supportive process childbearing should be. Instead, many modern women deal with unprecedented loneliness and lack of support. In past decades, a new mama was surrounded by mothers, aunts, and local community — all ready to care for mama and baby.

Once during my OB-GYN rotation, I encountered 15 family members inside the room of a mama I was preparing to deliver her baby. New mama was happy she had specifically requested to have her family there. She looked so comfortable allowing even grandpa and uncles to see the baby enter the world. It was beautiful and the cheers in the room illustrated robust support for mama. Because of the support, that mother probably recovered faster and possessed a better sense of well-being.

That was an ideal situation.

Many women have a much less stellar support experience.

Now it may seem obvious if you have a partner, involved parents, in-laws, aunts, and friends that you have your support all figured out. But you will need to play a more active role in the support you receive and don't allow people around you to offer passive support in how they think you need it. Take control and verbalize the unique form of support you may need. I remember feeling overwhelmed by all the offers for support; it was mostly for food, which was amazing and got us through. Looking back, I'd do a lot differently and I would have accepted offers of help and support.

For most, the responsibility for support lies with just the partner. That's a lot to take care of. Others may be fortunate to have supportive parents and friends. While others have no one, they feel safe to rely on for support.

Don't compare your support to others, yours may look very different. It may be disheartening to see your friend Sally, her mom, and grandma, all move in to support her for her first year of motherhood while you had no one to even bring you a meal and had to pay a mortgage in daycare costs.

Never assume only certain people can help or how they can help. The reality is we are in different times, and everyone is having to take care of themselves. We are having to work more to afford basic needs. So don't be above paying your mom or sister or aunt to help you with childcare rather than expect free childcare from them. There are no rules or expectations for support just honest assessment and conversations stating your needs and respecting how and if others can meet them.

Start building a social network, community, and making friends now.

With people having to move around more for work we are lonelier than ever. Also, we are being sold the false narrative that we don't need others, we are shown how to cut people out that no longer serve us but not how to add people that we can serve and can serve us in return. The art of community and friendships is lost for some. This starts way before you think about even getting pregnant, it is an essential part of your well-being and consequently wellness. As a coach I guide clients on the foundations of wellness and how cultivating healthy mutually supportive relationships is paramount because I personally have experienced the effects of poor relationships on my wellness.

Anatomy of An Emergency Support Squad

Any squad, even if it includes only one person, is better than none. However, this book will provide resources you can use in the hospital if you do not have a squad.

Even with the best squad, life happens. Some hospitals have horrible reception. You may not get a call out, or your friends and family are busy when you need them. Whatever the reason, know that you are not alone. You can build an emergency squad right there in the hospital. You just need to know who to ask for.

Don't have a squad? Locate the persons with the following roles:

- Charge nurse
- Nursing director
- Off shift nursing administrator
- Patient advocate
- Social worker

Know these roles and engage the people who have them.

Ideally, you should do this before you have any issues. These people are better trained to de-escalate and advocate for you as the patient, these leaders are also trained to balance your client/patient needs. In addition, these folks are empowered to make decisions that your floor staff cannot (such as obtaining additional equipment from other floors, and so on). They may also contact a different medical provider if you feel the ones caring for you are not appropriate. Remember, the "us against them" mentality and lack of trust can be a strong feeling and cause you to give up, so please isolate to only those involved and calmly ask, and have your squad calmly ask for more help.

Understanding Healthcare Roles

"Be your own healthcare advocate—get educated and understand the complexities of the system."
    —Mary Elizabeth Williams

IT'S OVERWHELMING to lack an understanding of the many people that may come and go in your hospital and clinic room. Some staff members are very busy and rushed and may skim through their explanation of who they are and what they do. This can leave you confused and decrease trust in the system.

Always confirm who someone is when they enter your room, and before they treat you. The person should have a badge and provide their name and job title. If you don't understand, always ask for more information.

For example, say, "I'm not familiar with that title. Can you explain your role on my care team, please?"

This is a quick way to build connection and trust. Be curious. Ask the person how long they have worked at the hospital. The staff should be happy to tell you all about themselves and the role they play, especially how they all work together to help you feel better. Some roles may provide unsolicited medical advice— you must understand who can help you clinically and filter out who you should rely on for specific medical information and guidance. For example, if a nurse gives you diagnosis and treatment options before you talk with the doctor, you can set a boundary and say, "I'm uncertain about this. I prefer to wait for my provider or doctor to discuss with me what this can be."

What is another reason to ensure you know who you are speaking to? You do not want to exhaust yourself giving your full story so many times that by the time your actual provider gets there you have fatigue, and you give a vague summary of why you are there.

While you receive care, always ask the role each person plays so you feel more in control. Write their names and titles in your journal and title as you may need to follow up with similar roles or specialties.

Common Hospital and Care Center Roles

Faculty

In healthcare faculty is a term used to refer to medical providers, usually doctors, physician associate (PAs), and advanced practice registered nurses (APRNs) who work in an academic hospital. An academic hospital is a hospital that is labeled as a teaching institution. These providers take part in research, teaching, training, and patient care.

Attending

A doctor who supervises the training and education of trainees such as medical residents, medical students, PA or APRN student interns. This person handles your overall care and is consulted either in person or by phone to discuss each case the trainee sees.

Resident

A doctor who is still in training, but has finished four years of medical school, so they have received the MD title (master) depending on the field. This person can be a resident for 3-7 or more years. They are chosen and employed by the hospital. They are always linked to an attending who supervises and teaches them. They can perform all areas of health care with varying level of supervision as they progress.

Medical Student

When in a hospital, this person has completed two years of medical school and now takes part in a variety of clinical rotations to practice and learn patient care. Medical students are always supervised and report to a clinician and/or resident. They aren't licensed. They can't prescribe medication or perform certain functions independently.

Intern

A resident during his very first year of training in a hospital after finishing four years of medical school. This person may still rotate within several subspecialties before they focus.

Fellow

After residents complete their resident training, they can choose to do a fellowship in a subspecialty of their choice for a few years. This person is also employed by the hospital and selected into a fellowship program. A fellow reports in person and/or remotely to a faculty and attending.

PA Student

When in a hospital, a physician associate student is completing his/her final year of clinical rotations, preparing to take their boards the next year. This person has completed one to two years of their medical school training.

Physician Associate

A licensed health care provider, also referred to as mid-level, but currently called an advanced practice provider (APP) who trains in a medical school format for approximately three years after receiving a bachelor's degree. This person earns a master's degree in their field but can also earn a doctorate in this or a related field. A PA is board-certified and must re-certify every ten years. PAs can be the lead healthcare provider and independently prescribe, diagnose, treat, and perform in any specialty of medicine. The role was created in 1967 to address health care gaps. All PAs have a supervising physician, but they are not required to supervise every case.

Nurse Practitioner - APRN

An advanced practice registered nurse who has completed a master's degree in nursing, at a nursing program. This person can assess patient needs, order, and interpret labs, imaging, diagnose and also can write prescriptions. APRNs also typically are supervised by a physician in their practice but can also work independently.

Consultant

The medical landscape includes many specialties. Specialists are people who have intensely studied certain areas of the body or disease groups.

Maternal Fetal Medicine

Your OB-GYN is a doctor who specializes in obstetrics and gynecology. An OB-GYN receives an additional 2-3 years of training in order to specialize in taking care of high-risk pregnancies, and so on. If you are high risk, you may have to consult with an MFM for some of your appointments and seen as well by your OB-GYN for your regular appointments if you are designated as high risk.

Charge Nurse

The lead nurse of a group of nurses in a particular ward or floor. This person acts in a supervisory way but may also care for nurses. They can be a good person to discuss any concerns with, as they are typically the most experienced nurse.

Support Roles

The following roles are support staff who assist nurses in varying degrees to provide care for patients. They typically have less education than nurses, but still play vital role in helping complete tasks in patient care.

LVN or LPN

Licensed vocational nurse or licensed practical nurse who has a license in an approved vocational nursing program. They report to a nurse or doctor and help with certain delegated tasks except administering meditation.

CNA

A certified nurse assistant who takes on basic tasks for patients. This person assists nurses with tasks like monitoring vital signs, feeding, dressing, and other approved delegated tasks. They cannot provide medications.

Other roles include medical assistant, nursing assistant, and medical technician. All require supervision.

Nurse Manager

An administrative nurse who leads a group of nurses to ensure all staff are providing safe and high reliable care. This person focuses on operations and can also be escalated to if needed.

Doula

A doula is not a health care professional but a trained companion who helps women through childbirth. Many are also trained to assist women through certain health care experiences such as miscarriage or death. They may also function as guides, advocates, and people who provide physical, emotional, and informational support.

Midwife

A trained health care professional, this person can be a registered nurse, or possess a bachelor's with specialized training. A midwife can safely care for women in labor independently, in a home, clinic or hospital setting, they can assess, anticipate, and manage some complications if they occur.

Medical or Nursing Director

A clinician whose role is to direct and oversee and ensure quality care in a particular department or division. They particularly ensure they oversee quality improvements projects, policy creation operations and supervise the care of other medical practitioners.

There are also nursing directors who perform similar roles but oversee the practice for groups of nurses. It is a good role to be aware of. You and your advocate can always communicate directly if you face issues with quality or policies. They can offer helpful insights and assist with resolution and practice improvement and correction.

Hospital Patient Advocate/Liaison/Representative/Care Manager/Ombudsman

All different titles to describe someone who provides neutral space to share any complaints, concerns, or problems. This person helps parties to find a problem resolution. Patient advocates are skilled at providing recourse to individuals and families about patients' rights and responsibilities. They help offer mediation for situations between patients and hospital staff till case is resolved. This person is a powerful ally in the event you need help navigating the healthcare system. It is required that one be available to patients 24/7. There are companies that offer independent patient advocacy services that have allegiance only to you and not affiliated with the hospital. As always, make sure there are no blind spots in their offer.

Social Worker

Social workers in medical settings are licensed professionals who can help patients address mental health issues and come up with information, resources on emotional, social, and financial needs that may arise because of their care or their illness. This is another powerful advocate because of their skills in communication and dealing with emotionally charged situations.

Case Manager

Case managers help patients with serious conditions who will require care and treatments even after their clinical stay. They are the liaison to help co-ordinate treatment and care option and smooth follow up and transition. For example, helping with transfer or set up of rehabilitation, and so on. Case managers typically possess fantastic coping skills to deal with stressful situations.

CREATING THE MODERN-DAY BABY SHOWER

"A baby shower should nurture and prepare a new mother for the journey ahead."
—Maya Angelou

IT TAKES A VILLAGE.

Preparing for baby's arrival is one of those events that can bring lots of anxiety to mama. The sheer number of items needed. The costs involved. The arrangements that need to be made while working. Wow! There aren't enough hours in the day to fit all the prep in. Anxiety can also exist for most moms who don't want to 'jinx' the pregnancy (due to fear of miscarriage or other first trimester complications) by getting ready too early. And so, preparations are left until the end when they can become even more difficult.

But there is one event all mamas love: the baby shower.

The baby shower is such a beautiful event. Picture mama smiling while surrounded by friends and family. A loving festivity with beautifully wrapped gifts. After the yucky symptoms of my first trimester, I spent many hours crafting a perfect registry requesting tons of products (most I used and some I never used). Later, I realized most of the gifts I could have ordered in the future, when I truly confirmed a need for them.

When I planned my baby shower, it was a scary time that occurred during the height of the pandemic. I knew I wouldn't get to enjoy the typical baby shower being surrounded physically by family and friends. Still, my sisters and friends threw a huge virtual shower and my husband, and I felt so loved. We could celebrate with more people than we could if we had held a typical baby shower in our home. We could celebrate our twins with our amazing friends and family across the globe. We were so grateful. Our registry was completely bought for us.

When I consider my own baby shower, and as I take part in other showers, I have more questions.

- Does mama really have everything she will need to be supported?
- Does she have emotional support in the form of advice or information?
- Does she have support in the form of positive affection and social interaction?

When I had my baby shower, all the items I thought I'd need focused on the babies. There were many infant-related products, but minimal mommy products to support the immediate postpartum—such as bras and special balms for chapped nipples from breastfeeding. The focus was the same throughout my pregnancy—the things I ate before and during and after delivery all focused on baby. I don't think I'm the only mother who has noticed this.

But think for a moment. What would it look like to include key items for mama on the registry? What if mama received the type of supplies that enable her to thrive during pregnancy? What does planning that type of shower look like?

What if we had a mama *and* baby registry?

It seems we are hard wired to think only the baby will have

needs. That the baby is the most important thing. Okay, the baby is important, but we still need to challenge ourselves to consider mama's importance. Without mama's survival, baby's chance of survival is lower. Research proves this. Not only is baby affected if we don't ensure mama thrives, our families, communities, economy, and world suffer every time we lose a mama.

How can we change the way we create the baby registry? Or how do we reimagine the baby shower (or baby sprinkle for moms with children already)? It is such a pivotal event to truly support mama and baby. How do we create an event that not only plans how our babies will be supported and nourished but also equally puts mom and her well-being at the center?

Mama should have tools to assess herself early when she's not feeling well. It's the year 2023 and we now have so many more biological monitoring gadgets. Note that some providers discourage getting tools to help you track vital signs because they don't want mama to worry needlessly. However, certain tools can teach patients to empower themselves to track and follow along their own physiologic readings. They can help mama know when to reach out. Please note, the tools below are not exhaustive, as always discuss with your provider and please calibrate your device with your provider's office for the sake of accuracy.

MAMA SAVING REGISTRY

Would you like to build the world's first *Mama Saving Registry?* Here is what it should include:

- A health/pregnancy journal — There is no more important time in a woman's life where a simple journal could be a safe place for her to write her fears, joys, hopes, dreams. With a pregnancy journal she can track her thoughts day by day, including how she is feeling — all so she can also share with her provider as needed.

- A blood pressure machine — I recommend any mom with advanced maternal age, or with other risk factors such as obesity, history of high blood pressure, or heart conditions always have a working blood pressure machine. Discuss with your provider to see how it compares to the machine in their clinic.

- A heart rate monitor — During my postpartum period, I had a day when I felt bad during a drive back from the NICU. I felt exhausted, but I checked my heart rate and decided not to sleep off the bad feeling. My heart rate was very low for me, and the reading told me I needed to seek care immediately and not go to sleep, which could have been fatal. So, I'd rather you have more information than less. You need to know if your heart rate is abnormally too fast or too slow and this needs to be tracked up to one year postpartum. Thankfully, a lot of these devices are easily got from your local CVS or Walgreens, with different price ranges and is also now built into some watches, the apple watch for example can give you a heart rate, your oxygen saturation and even a snapshot of your heart rhythm.

- A pulse oximeter — This is a small clip-like device that attaches to your finger. You use it to see if your blood is well oxygenated.

- A good working thermometer

- If diabetic, must have a working glucose monitor

- An abdominal binder if having a c-section — This was something I had to request but it did wonders for my post operation pain control. It was a lifesaver.

- An Apple watch though expensive could be a great tool that does a lot of the assessment above like heart rate, oxygen saturation and even an EKG. As long as mama remembers to wear it, the future is tools that encourage us to assess ourselves so that we reach out for help sooner if needed.

All of this is to move to a world where we teach mothers to be active in their own timely clinical assessment and play a vital part in early recognition instead of one that is based on avoidance and ignorance. I truly believe this will improve the patient experience of mothers and increase their confidence. I wish even as a clinician I could have been more prepared for my appointments especially in the second or third trimester.

Vital signs are just a snapshot. The more data, the better the story about your health.

THE BEST NEW MAMA CALENDAR EVER

If I host a baby shower again in the future, there will be flowers and treats and decorations. There will also be an amazing, beautiful calendar with dates, rows, and columns for guests to sign up for labeled shifts such as:

- FaceTime with mama
- Cooking
- Laundry
- Taking mama for a walk
- Maintaining the calendar
- Checking on mama by text or by phone

Imagine if people gave that level of support during the baby's first year!

Some of you might think, *No way. I couldn't ask that of my friends and family!*

I hope, from what you have read here, that you understand how important it is for you to allow others to support you. The support is vital for your health and your baby's health.

ALTERNATE REGISTRIES

Use alternative registries to set up funds for doula care and a night nurse. You might even schedule walks/playdates, meals to be delivered using amazing platforms like so kind registry.org. you can ask for services, gentle used hand-me-downs from friends.

Some of us have very skilled and talented friends with skills they can happily share. Dog sitting/walking is another type of support that is helpful for the mama who has a pet. All attention is on baby those first few weeks, so offering to keep the dog or if you live close by offering to take the dog for a walk is incredible help.

Some of us use home cleaning services. Talk to a cleaning team and ask them to provide however many cleaning sessions for the new mother. Discuss the importance of wearing masks and even using fragrance-free and natural products where possible since there is a newborn. All you have to do is provide mama with the number when she is ready to use it. If out of service range, call some local cleaners and offer some options. The idea is to make it as simple as possible and easy for use.

Do not be afraid to show up for mothers especially those with low support. Listen and observe. For mothers who work or have poor relationships or no network, book that new mom support group for her if she hasn't and hold her accountable for setting it. Make sure when baby comes those support systems are in place. Offer to drive mama to groups/appointments— even virtual or telephone support is better than nothing just do and apologize later. Food is great but so is physical support.

I challenge all other future baby shower (or baby sprinkle) planners to use the suggestions and recommendations to plan a more balanced baby shower or sprinkle that will help mama thrive. Multiple baby blankets and stuffed animals are super cute, but they may not be what mama truly needs to survive the first few months and year after baby gets here.

PART THREE

THE POWER OF
JOURNALS AND STORIES

Journaling

"The written word can be the most powerful form of healing."
　—Patti Digh

YOU DON'T HAVE to only journal about your medical history. Mama, I urge you to try the habit of journaling before, during, and after your journey into motherhood. Journaling gives you space to get out, explore and reflect on the things you feel in your heart and head. There is no more active and more emotional time than during pregnancy and as a new parent. There will be a myriad of thoughts, emotions, beliefs that you will need to process, and journaling can be powerful.

Science proves that in postpartum, journaling, also known as expressive writing, can reduce stress, symptoms of depression, and post-traumatic symptoms. It improves quality of life and lowers healthcare costs. Writing about your thoughts and feelings at least 15 minutes a day was found to have amazing effects.

Grab that journal and create a safe space to connect with yourself unapologetically. Let go of pent-up frustration and anger. Share your deepest thoughts and fears, without being afraid of judgement. Please make time for this, as a busy mom of twins I kept my journal—full disclosure—close to the toilet so I would journal right after I went for a bathroom break to decompress anxious thoughts I was having or jot down feelings I needed to express.

Journaling is rewarding. You can look back on your entries and see how far you have come.

Journal Ideas

You can start journaling now. You don't have to wait. Here are a few things you can enter:

- Questions to ask your doctor during your next appointment. This is helpful, as you forget more easily when pregnant. You can also keep an electronic version of this in your phone.Your symptoms, vital signs, and medications.
- Notes from your doctors visits.
- Your symptoms, vital signs, and medications.
- Write notes during your doctor's visits so you don't forget
- Your gratitude lists.
- Milestones for you and baby.
- Items you need for your pregnancy.
- Items you have received for your pregnancy
- Parenting tips, advice, and styles you are considering.
- Reflections about your self-care the day before: what you ate, drank, your exercise, and meditation. This list will help keep you accountable to yourself. You can make a checklist for yourself care because during postpartum it can feel so hard to do the basics. Shower-check, eat a nutritious meal-check, do a 5–10-minute exercise or walk-check, did I talk to an adult about something other than babies. Check. Did you get at least 4-5 hours of sleep?

- Pregnancy moments and memories you don't want to forget.

JOURNAL PROMPTS FOR CARE AND SUPPORT

- What support do you need during this postpartum period?
- What strategies do you have to cope with postpartum emotions and stress?
- How have you reached out for help when you need it? If not, how can you reach out for help?
- How does receiving support help your health and wellbeing as well as babies?
- What have been the most helpful sources of support for you?
- How can you create a supportive postpartum environment for yourself at home and in your community?
- How can friends and family members support you during this postpartum period?
- How can you prioritize your own needs while also caring for your family?
- What activities bring you joy and help you to re-connect with yourself?
- How can you stay connected to other new moms and find support?
- How do you ensure you are getting enough rest and recovery time?
- What warning signs should prompt you to seek medical care?
- How can you create a plan for seeking medical care if needed?
- What have you done to ensure you have access to quality health care?

- How can you advocate for yourself to receive the best care possible? Or even a second opinion?
- How can you seek support to help you through any health challenges?
- What is your experience in seeking health care? Has it been positive or negative? What happened? How did it make me feel?
- Have you been a victim of racial discrimination or any other form for any of my identities, gender, sexual orientation, religion, disability?
- Have I healed from a negative incident as such?
- What can I do to heal from the incident as I go forward so my care is not affected?

JOURNAL PROMPTS FOR POSTPARTUM

- What emotions did you experience after giving birth? Did any surprise you and why?
- How have your relationships changed since becoming a mother?
- What have you learned about yourself since becoming a mother?
- How have you managed the challenges of motherhood? Where are you struggling and what skills can you draw from?
- What has been the most rewarding experience of being a mother?
- How has your spirituality / faith impacted your motherhood journey?
- What has been the biggest surprise of motherhood?
- How has your view of the world changed since becoming a mother?
- How has your level of self-care changed since becoming a mother?

- How have your values and beliefs shifted since becoming a mother?
- What advice would you give to a new mother?
- How has the experience of motherhood changed your life?

STORYTELLING

"There is no greater agony than bearing an untold story inside of you."

—Maya Angelou

WHAT IS STORYTELLING?

WHEN I THINK OF STORYTELLING, I always think of the stories my family and friends told while I grew up in Africa. Some were funny, superstitious, and scary. Typically, they evoked a feeling, drove home pearls of knowledge, and promoted connection to our roots and culture.

Story telling provides the opportunity to show and communicate our world to another person—to convey how we see, feel, and experience from our own lens. Story telling is even more impactful when the person you are telling the story to differ from you or does not experience life the same way you do, if the person's race, culture, gender, religion, or sexual orientation differs from yours.

As a clinician, I didn't realize just how much this plays a part in my role every day. When I walk into a room to talk to a patient, I'm asking them to tell a story about their health—a tale about what brings them there. In a nutshell: their health story.

Storytelling is a double-edged sword. First, you must be mindful of the story—the full story. When I prepared to welcome my twins to the world, I didn't have the complete story. Even as a clinician who had seen horrendous complications and lost a dear friend, I still approached my pregnancy without the entire story about the risks involved with childbirth. I was oblivious to the effects of so many other factors that exist in the hospital I chose, timing, my race, my background, and so on.

THE POWER OF STORYTELLING

Stories are powerful because they can shift our perception, give us the motivation to make change, and reduce suffering from the pearls of wisdom embedded in them. I wish I had learned earlier in life the power of storytelling and the art form. As someone who values arts and creativity, becoming a mother opened my eyes to the power of storytelling. When I prepared to welcome my twin girls into the world, many stories from other twin moms gave me courage and hope that despite the pandemic state my husband and I could survive this challenging feat. As a student, clinician, I read a lot of fact-based text about pregnancy and parenting multiples. But it was the stories that resonated the most. The stories helped me connect the most with the information and help me see how I could apply the information to my life despite any difference between the storyteller and myself.

WHY DOES IT MATTER?

When a patient tells me the story of what brings them in, I try to visualize based on my medical training. The patient takes me on a journey—one that requires empathy to feel and experience the issue that brought them to the appointment. I also have to tell my story to this patient in a manner that fosters relationship and creates trust. I use stories to persuade or enable patients to connect better with the recommendations or advice being given.

Earlier I talked about how this story can be from a very different lens than mine based on their gender, or their culture. It requires me to fight against any assumptions I may have, truly silence them, and remain in the moment. This is a skill of listening to get the information needed to take care of my patient. I have honed this skill for over 15 years.

Achieving the goal behind it is a skill, especially when the goal is to inspire someone to do what is necessary to take care of you appropriately. Storytelling between a patient and provider is the highest form of the art and requires attention and guidance. Learning the power of telling your story and experiences confidently is how we begin to grow and fix this system.

In these next few pages I will share with you three pivotal stories of myself and others that highlight the reason I felt inspired and called to write this book, I hope these stories don't instill fear but instill power, strength and connection to these women who could be you, your sister, friend, cousin, neighbor and you feel empowered to carry and share their story to learn from it, save someone else and reduce their suffering.

MY STORY

As an immigrant, I am grateful of the opportunities afforded to me by living in America. One of those opportunities is access to reliable healthcare.

My journey as a patient began long before I was a clinician. It began in high school when I noticed a large lump in my breast. Though it was incredibly expensive, my family were grateful to find a good team to evaluate and plan to remove the mass. I would have more lumps and consequently more surgeries, but I was blessed to feel heard and understood by my medical teams. My parents were always satisfied with the level of care I was given. In fact, I would describe my care as exceptional, except for the financial burden, everyone knew their role. When they interacted with me, they did it with the utmost respect, like a well-oiled machine. The spaces were clean and organized. To a high schooler, nothing seemed out of place. Nothing looked like it could ever be wrong. In some ways, I assumed the high price of insurance and copayments guaranteed the high level of care I was accustomed to receiving. This type of healthcare is my wish for every person who presents to any hospital in this great country regardless of their skin color, sexual orientation, or socio-economic status, one full of the utmost trust and transparency. In fact, being such a young patient confirmed that I wanted a career in healthcare. I never hesitated to share that with my doctors or nurses. They would flash me smiles and say, "Well, when you are ready, you call me, and I'll show you the ropes." The care I received as a teenager influenced my decisions in the career, I find myself today.

Therefore, being no stranger to the hospital setting both as a clinician and a patient, I was very confident in my ability to navigate the system. When my husband and I found out we were having twins in the beginning of 2020, we were ecstatic, shocked, scared, and happy. So many emotions all at once. After all, we had enough things to worry about. There was the pandemic that was causing mass hysteria. There was my health as ours had been a journey. We had prepared ourselves for the realization a lot of women face—that maybe we wouldn't be parents, or that it would take several tries and in vitro fertilization (IVF). I had undergone two surgical procedures before the year we conceived. One for a thyroid autoimmune condition and, the other for large fibroids that required removal.

All this to say that I was not confident I would ever become a mother. Instead, I threw myself into my work and vowed to learn as much as possible through studying public health and social work.

Imagine my shock that day in my OB-GYN clinic as I learned the symptoms leading to my positive pregnancy test were NOT symptoms from my previous surgeries or other issues. Being a healthcare provider, there's a feeling of dread and anxiety that can consume you when you are going through a health-related experience because of your knowledge of health complications that can occur. You start off knowing so much more than the average patient. Sometimes I argue this is not a good thing. It's like holding a small WebMD in your brain. A WebMD that is inappropriately anxiety-provoking. Most patients without medical backgrounds experience a lucky protective naivety to the in-depth framework of medicine.

I was already thinking at appointment number one about every maternal complication or death I had ever heard about. I planned and plotted how I would be extra vigilant about any early warnings or symptoms. For me, I already knew the differential diagnosis for all symptoms. I thought if I saw light spotting or bleeding, well my brain would think, this could be nothing or it could be sub-chorionic hemorrhage of the uterus, placenta abruption, or something else. The list went on and on. Differential diagnosis is the term we use in the medical fields to describe the alternative causes or reasons a patient is having certain symptoms they report before we settle on the diagnosis that reveals itself after getting labs and studies. In fact, in an appointment with my OB-GYN, I shared the loss of my dear friend Liz. And I think in some ways it changed the course of my care. It made my provider more vigilant. We held discussions I doubt we would have had if I hadn't shared my own medical story and the story about how Liz passed away.

My OB-GYN made me feel at ease. She didn't dismiss any of my concerns. She was very knowledgeable. She sat eye-to-eye with me, not towering, or with arms folded. She said we would work together, and she was honest about the risks. We planned as best we could for them. We talked about things like my risk factors for pre-eclampsia, which was really the only complication for which I might be at risk. Not for the reasons I now know, mostly because I had lost a friend to it. I wasn't aware of my personal risks.

As I neared my third trimester, I realized someone on my OB's team who I didn't know or have a relationship with might deliver my babies. So, I asked for the names of those on her team. I researched them and she assured me everyone on the staff was extremely capable and would do a great job.

Secretly, I felt falsely protected—safe in the knowledge and background of my healthcare team that would protect me before, during, and after childbirth. After all, I had spent five years working in an ER and other hospitals. I felt very confident that if a problem came up, I would have no problem stating my concerns and having the medical staff hear me. After all, I spoke their lingo. I was one of them!

Navigating this new fear-based world through all that chaos, I did what I could to focus on the two miracles growing inside me. I did my best to stay away from the news, and let my husband keep me posted on important updates. I knew stress and anxiety would not foster a successful pregnancy, so I practiced yoga to stay healthy and reduce my anxiety levels. As I grew bigger, we celebrated every week and milestone. It became difficult to move. Going from the couch to the kitchen seemed like a minor feat in and of itself. Somewhat like climbing a hill with a growing log strapped to your belly. My 5-foot frame struggled to complete even the most mundane tasks by 30 weeks. I was grateful when we were forced to be at home and not in a bustling busy world. Another silver lining for us, the pandemic in a way allowed us to really focus on our family and prepare to care for our girls. Though we couldn't enjoy physical contact with friends and family, we felt supported in so many other ways: phone calls, meal drop off, and being showered with gifts from our registry.

As my husband and I prepared to celebrate making it to 32 weeks, we were confident we had no reason to worry. We thought we would keep up our healthy daily routines. We had planned to do a C-section in 2-3 weeks to reduce my risk of complications from the recent surgery I'd had.

One night I was making a meal in the kitchen and in hindsight had been on my feet a lot that day organizing the nursery. I felt a gush of fluid flow downward as I turned the curry I was preparing. I knew immediately it was "go time." I screamed for my husband who was grilling in our apartment courtyard. He sprinted once he heard we had to go!

We were less than 10 minutes from the hospital, so I was wheeled to triage in no time. I felt a lot of pressure in my lower pelvis, and it was uncomfortable. Once past triage, I had to get a COVID test, which was more painful than the labor pains, I thought. I was relieved it was negative.

Everything else was a blur from then forward. I figured I'd be on bed rest and would spend two weeks in the hospital to give the babies more time to develop. It turned out that was a big NO. I had to deliver.

My doc calmly reassured me, "You did great to get them to this point."

We were in the operating room quickly—a place I was oddly familiar with both as patient and clinician. Before I knew it, I could practically walk through every surgical step in my head as I felt my belly being manipulated and moved around. I had assisted quite a few C-sections in my training and residency as a physician associate. My focus was that my babies were okay. As I felt the doctor reach in and grasp baby A, I held my breath. I was waiting for the sound everyone in the room waited for. Then it came. A loud shrilling cry. Tears came running down my face and I stilled for the second grasp for baby B. Two minutes later, I felt the pressure and then yes, that sweet cry that told everyone in the room they were at least stable and had functioning lungs. I got a glimpse of them as they whisked them off to be stabilized and transferred to the NICU.

I told my husband to stay with the babies and follow them. That was the beginning of my postpartum anxiety as I was nervous about theft or a switch at birth, which I had heard stories of as a clinician.

Then it was quiet. I was wheeled to a PACU. I held back hot tears of frustration and sadness. I wasn't able to hold my babies immediately. Disappointment flooded me—this was not the typical birth experience I was familiar with. The birth experiences I'd witnessed included so many people in the rooms—moms, spouses, dads, uncles, and aunties. And even more people in the waiting room. The realization of the future isolation a necessary part to keep us and our babies safe from COVID set in.

It felt like ten hours before I was wheeled to the NICU to get a glimpse of my babies. I had not visited the inside of many NICUs, so my experience was foggy. I was shocked at the number of tubes and lines hooked to the girls' bodies. Sadness washed over me, and I cried because I couldn't help but wonder if it was my fault. I was also triggered by the noise of the vital sign alarms, which seemed to go off constantly and would send terrifying chills down my spine even when the alarms were for other children. I had not prepared for this part especially, the NICU experience, seeing my babies so helpless, the frantic pace. The rules that seemed to be made and revised daily, as everyone was figuring out the pandemic.

I would have slept on a floor next to the twins' incubator if they would have allowed me. Every time I was wheeled away from them it felt like a piece of my heart was being torn away.

I had researched one of the best things I could do for my babies in the NICU was skin to skin contact. Amazing literature detailed how "kangaroo care" shortened hospital stays and helped babies thrive. So, I was sold, and I asked to do it—lines and tubes and all. I didn't see too many other parents do it, but I trusted the research. In shifts, my husband and I gave them as much close contact as we could.

The long hours in the NICU took a toll on me. We were doing 10-hour shifts since we weren't allowed to leave the hospital and come back because of the pandemic. Instead, we stayed as long as we could before we drove home, gloomy, and unsure of what to do with ourselves. It was an odd existence. We were nervous about the state of the country, world, and our babies all at the same time.

I would go to sleep at night hearing the loud alarms of the NICU in my head. Wondering about my babies, I'd set alarms every 3 hours to check on their status with the night nurse, charting their growth. Every gram gained meant we were getting closer to take them home!

Two weeks into our NICU stay and I felt unwell—tired and felt short of breath. I attributed it to the long hours and the C-section scar, but then it got worse. I used my blood pressure machine and my heart rate monitor at home as I felt something was wrong. It felt like pressure on my chest and like if I slept my heart might stop. My heart rate was very low, and I knew I had to seek help immediately. My husband dropped me at the front of the hospital where my kids were. I figured it was the best place to go, as I figured this was closely related to my delivery. Medical staff wheeled me in alone because of COVID policy. On arrival, I was triaged, and I shared my history as clearly as I could.

The nurse was friendly. She smiled and said, "Having twins can be stressful and cause anxiety. You are probably just worried."

I remained silent and stared at her. I glanced at my low heart rate and knew it wasn't an anxious reaction. That I had just had twins should have caused her to jump into action and not speculate immediately without a workup that this may just be my 'nerves'.

The doctor walked in and gave me a similar statement. Though I clearly had a low heart rate, he didn't think it was that bad. He thought it could be followed up on. No tests had been done. They were nice. They weren't rude, but it appeared as though they were both being aggressively persuasive oddly. My usual ability to advocate for myself was dampened to my surprise. As I reflect, I underestimated the effects of postpartum on my mental state. I wanted to believe them badly. I was tired and wanted to be anywhere but there. Maybe this was in my head?

Thankfully, I snapped out of it and decide to call my friend, Dr. Hold. Dr. Hold was an OB-GYN, and also my friend Liz's brother. He had been part of all our friends' support squads, without us realizing it. He had always been there if we ever had questions regarding our OB care. Fortunately, I could reach him, and I gave him the scenario. He validated I was right to go the hospital, and he told me to demand a workup before any decisions were made.

After discussing it with the doctor, he reluctantly agreed to get the labs. I waited. At least I was relieved something was being done to help me figure out what was going on. Even today, I'm still in shock that this ER didn't have a working differential for me. All they could offer was an attitude of, "We're not sure what's going on with you, so we'll assume you're making it up."

After what seemed like forever and a bunch of tests, the doctor came back in and shared that yes, my heart markers, and liver and kidney numbers were elevated.

"Hope you are happy. You bought yourself an admission," he said. It was a quick comment. His body barely entered the room. Neither *the doctor nor nurse was as chatty anymore. They just quietly got me ready to go to the floor. I wish that was where this story ended, but the decisions the doctor made would follow me unto the floor.*

When I arrived at my bed, happy to be on the floor, I expected a flurry of activity to understand what was happening. I hoped to see doctors, providers, and a specialist. However, it was about 11:00 PM by the time I entered my room, and in this hospital no consultant would be available until the next morning. The room was bare, with no monitor.

I turned to my nurse. "I am here for low heart rate. How will you know when my heart rate drops lower than is safe?

She said, "Sorry, but the doctor didn't order that type of monitoring for you. He said just to check you every four hours."

I was floored. All those negative feelings slammed into me once more. My eyes pleaded with my nurse.

She was unmoved. "There is no one available right now to make any changes."

I let my husband and family know my status, then I called my sister on the phone. She said, "I can't let you fall asleep unless I know you are monitored!"

I was about to give up arguing with the nurse, but my sister helped me see how stupid it was to not have a monitor in my room now that was only going to be checked every four hours. So, I stayed strong, and she continued arguing with us.

That this was how this hospital operated based on orders from the ER, my ER doctor, and his doubt of what was going on still haunted me. Also, I was in a hospital that, unless I was dying actively, my care was on pause until the morning when consultants would be available.

Finally, we asked to speak with the nurse's supervisor. She came in and we calmly reported why we needed to have telemetry, which is supervised monitoring so someone other than me would be notified if I got in trouble with my heart rate. She was understanding and apologized profusely. She said she would run up to the ICU and grab a portable telemetry for me and agreed I should not have been put on a regular floor. She returned quickly and connected me to the monitor. That night I had two episodes where my heart rate dipped into the 40-

50's and I was checked on by the ICU staff. Then morning came, and the hospital transformed. The cardiologist and a flurry of doctors came in. I took tests for my heart, CT scans, and more labs. The whole time, everyone said they weren't sure what was going on since I had already had my babies. They put me on medications that helped regulate my heart and blood pressure. Thankfully, I was stable enough to be discharged after two days of medications.

I am sharing my story because I hope it sheds some light on how we can work together to improve our system. Also, I'd like to help another mother like you notice some of our health care system failures so you can be more prepared. This story and others I have been a part of in maternal morbidity and maternal mortality have haunted me and led me to writing this book.

I was the face of a maternal complication incident.

I never thought it could happen to me.

Even with my education and experience, I never realized my race could trump all of that. I know for certain my race was the cause for dismissing my symptoms. Looking back and reading the statistics was chilling.

I almost became a statistic.

LIZ'S STORY

Liz was more like a sister than a friend to many. Every day I feel so blessed that I got to spend the time and bond with her as much as I did. Our bond was over creativity. I think she was one of the first few people who saw in me something I didn't see in myself. I had a powerful urge to have a creative outlet and maybe even dare to make a business of it. Before that I would help design and style any events that I could. She was always so enamored with my creations and would visit and look at my creations or my process and tools. She loved being creative, and most of all she loved to share it with her friends and community, something I was not very good at.

To this day she inspires me. She was fearless in saying, "Hey everyone come on! Let's just have a great time!" Liz celebrated

*everything with so much passion, her dog birthdays, her friends'
birthdays or achievements, Liz had the most amazing parties. Her
favorite was during Halloween. I have never seen someone get so into
the spirit of Halloween. Liz literally transformed her home, and we all
looked forward to her parties. When you walked through the doors of
Liz home, on one of her Halloween parties, you were immediately
transformed into a different world, Liz would have painstakingly
changed all the photographs in the frames in her entire home to spooky
creepy ones. Every corner of her home was spookily decorated and
really, as an adult it took us all back to being a kid again. This
immigrant kid who never got to grow up was probably the most
impressed, because it was all so new to me.*

*She would make meals and desserts labeled perfectly with spooky
names like dead fingers that were fries, and so on. And the pièce de
résistance was a gorgeous Halloween candy bar, with very fun spooky
labels and colored flavors you can imagine.*

*I'll admit Liz was a friend I had known about more years than we
actually got to spend together. Her childhood friends were my college
friends and our paths rarely crossed as I was away in graduate school,
or she was away when I'd be visiting.*

*We laughed because every time I'd be with our friends in common
and they'd be like you know Liz right and I'd be like yes, I know her by
name, but we had actually never met, and we would always be so
shocked at the fact that our paths had not crossed even though we heard
and knew about each other so much for years on end.*

*A little side story. During my job as a physician associate working
in neurosurgery, we occasionally would manage patients who had
sustained significant complications during their delivery, such as a
stroke and or a brain bleed. We would work with residents to manage
them, and occasionally I'd manage them with a young resident who
worked on the OB-GYN team. For almost a year or more, a resident
that I later would find out was actually Liz's brother, Michael, was a
part of my support squad. He helped me feel heard and seen.*

*The synchronicities were abundant. It was like we were making
up for all the lost time that our lives were in parallel. I enjoyed*

planning out her Halloween party candy buffet and picking out the beautiful mason and apothecary jars to display them, ribbons. It was like watching a kid in a candy store. Her eyes and her whole self would come alive with so much excitement. And I also looked in awe because I couldn't imagine how she found time to put so much effort and love into a Halloween event, which she would plan months in advance. I was so fortunate to see her process. I loved that she trusted me almost immediately and had so much faith in my design and creative abilities. She always thought she owed me so much to pick my brain creatively, but she never knew that I learned and watched in awe her capacity to trust, be open, connect with others, and advocate. She was the first person who showed me advocacy by watching her every year get so many of us and even strangers riled up to support the annual scope walk in memory of her dear late friend, Donna. We would walk and have a great big brunch together. She did this every year with as much or more gusto than the last, even when pregnant.

She enjoyed designing her home, and I knew when she became a mom it would be a joy to see her put that level of enjoyment in nurturing and raising a child. That love for design and creativity was in her cooking. She loved to cook and the common thread for her was to foster connection; she used her creativity, love of home making to make her home an inviting and comfortable oasis, for her family, friends, and strangers. She would not just have big events at her home but also little intimate dinners to allow for even more connection for her and her friends.

I'll never forget the most impactful conversation I had with my dear friend when I asked her what she saw herself doing in the future. We all knew we wanted to be married and have a family, but we were all in jobs. We had dreams, and I wanted to know based on her amazing job in hotel and restaurant management, where she saw herself. I braced myself because she was accomplished and high achieving. I expected her to want her own hotel, or to be a hotel director. She smiled at me and answered with the most confidence I've ever met anyone in their twenties answer such a question.

She said, "I'm only working till I have a child. I just want to be a good mom and raise my child."

I was so impressed with her answer. She unequivocally knew what and who she wanted to be, and she set about working to fulfill that dream. I envied her because my answer to that question to this day still falters. I knew that if I ever had daughters, I wanted them to feel safe to always pursue their dream no matter what just like Liz.

Liz shared she was pregnant at her annual incredible Halloween party, and she went all out. She never celebrated in a small way. She lived her life in a big way and made all her friends feel so special and honored. She celebrated life in a way I can only aspire to. We all lined up to find out the announcements, and she had made a skeleton t-shirt with a baby and the due date.

As the months passed, our excitement for her and her son Evan grew. We had celebrated her baby shower two weeks before her due date. At the shower, I asked Liz, with a worried look on my face, about her swelled hands and face. She admitted her hand hurt and she couldn't close it or hold her pen. That was actually the third time I had brought up my concern about her swelling. It was all I could see, otherwise her pregnancy was unremarkable. After our last talk, she promised me she would talk to her doctor. After the first time I shared concern, she stated she was checked, and that all was fine per her doctor and that she did not have pre-eclampsia.

I will regret this till my last day that I didn't push her. That I didn't ask her to go to the ER during that baby shower. Or that I didn't put her in my car and drive her to the ER myself. I kept asking if her doctor knew about the swelling.

"Yes. All is fine," Liz told me.

Monday arrived, and Liz was at home when she began having headaches. She took Tylenol, but without relief. She took her blood register, but her machine didn't register. The pre-natal class she had taken taught her that headaches were a normal sign of pregnancy at the end.

She took a nap and sadly sustained a seizure.

That seizure took her, and baby Evan's, lives.

That day is marked in the hearts of all her family and friends. It still shocks us to this day. I remember the night it happened like it was yesterday. We had exchanged a few texts to meet to get items and photos from the shower. I had just gotten off an evening shift in the emergency room where I worked and was talking with a friend in the parking lot. My phone rang. It was my best friend. A sick feeling filled my stomach. I was afraid to answer, so I just stared at it.

The friend who stood beside me asked why I wasn't picking up.

I said, "I'm afraid of the message I think this call may be about."

My best friend called time after time, and I knew. I just knew. I dragged myself to the car, took the call, and listened to the devastating news.

Liz was gone. As was her baby Evan. To this day I can see her holding him in her arms as we laid her to rest. The amazing daughter, sister, friend, wife, and mother whose impact we continue to feel today.

I'm so grateful her family is letting me share her story, as I know it will continue to help so many other women. Just like it saved my life when I began my journey to motherhood.

At her funeral, a fellow friend helped me remember that Liz was one person who had learned all that was needed in life. It just was her time is what we tell ourselves to make sense of her senseless death. Her wisdom and bravery was unparalleled.

Juliet's Story

It was 1987. I was four years old going on five years old. We were playing on the narrow but long yard of my grandmother Maria's with my giant snails and beetle collection, feeding them lettuce and racing them against each other. Smiling, screaming, and excited in the carefree child-like wonder. I heard my grandma call out to us to come to her. I perked up immediately and run to her. My grandmother didn't like being made to wait, so when she called, you came running.

When I reached her, she said, "Your mom is here. Go and say hi."

In my then almost 5-year-old brain, the title didn't quite register. I hadn't seen her in a while. Months maybe even a year for me life was

149

moving at a much faster pace. In some ways, I wasn't sure who I'd be seeing. I recall now that walk to the gate was a long one as I wasn't quite sure who was being introduced to me as mom. I walked with my two siblings to the large, closed gate. I recognized her, but not in an 'I know her' way. More like, 'she looks very nice. I like her and she seems familiar to me.' She was pretty. She smelled like flowers. She hugged me and my siblings exaggeratedly. She held us tight like she never wanted to leave. The visit was brief. She said, 'I love you' and 'are you ok' over and over. We just looked at her in wonder and awe, not understanding why we were visiting someone so nice through a gate.

Then the visit was cut short. It was time to go. I realized she had been driven by another lady. Also, the visit was being monitored. My caretaker/nanny was right there. Also, our security guard for our compound, everyone watching intently, like our safety at any point would be compromised. The message it sent was that this woman was not to be trusted, not with our well-being or safety. I wasn't sure how to act; I thought I'd make someone mad if I was too excited to see her. I'd betray my grandma, who was home to me, if I hugged and was too excited to see this woman, I was being told was my mother. So, all she got were sheepish grins and a limp existence in her arm when she hugged.

When it was clear from everyone around it was time to go, she didn't let go. That's when the nanny and gateman moved in, and gently and slowly started prying her away from her tight embrace on us.

She pleaded, "No, no, no, leave me alone. Don't take them!"

Her words turned to cries.

The cries turned to screams.

My siblings and I watched her being carried away, out of the gate to the car. I locked gazes with her screaming eyes, hands outstretched, her friend grabbing her waist and moving her to the gate. Tears started rolling down my eyes. I didn't understand any of it, but I was very sad that she was sad. It hurt me a lot that she was so upset. I wanted her to stop crying. I knew in that moment that she shouldn't be leaving. She should be with us...but she wasn't. She didn't feel safe because *everyone acted like she wasn't. But I didn't know why. Not until much later.*

My mother's name is Juliet. Her mom died when she was 15 years old. During childbirth, while having her 7th baby, she died of bleeding. Stories of my maternal grandmother were passed on from my Aunt Gladys. Aunt Gladys shared that my grandmother was an incredible trader and businesswomen who could leave a legacy and wealth for her children in real estate and businesses.

My first solid visual memories of my own mom were through a large wrought-iron gate.

Any previous memories felt like dreams though real, whether that was her singing, cooking puffs for us to take to the zoo, or making us eat tomatoes, which I hated as a toddler. I don't have many memories of her—the ones I have I can fit them in both palms. Still, I treasure them. I think of them often now that she is no longer here. My memories solidify around age four, which was when we went to live with my grandmother.

The gate was intended to protect us from her.

I understand now. All of it was to protect us from an unknown, unpredictable, and poorly misunderstood taboo. It took a village to care for us, keep us safe, educated, and fed. All to fill the gap of not having a mother.

All this happened during a time when conscious parenting was not a thing. After all, the divorce had been final, and she had not gotten custody because of her mental health. To me it was pure and utter confusion. Why were her visits so brief? Why were the hugs so short? Why did she have to be dragged away by the person she visited with? Why was security holding her as she kicked, screamed, and reached for her children? My siblings and I would stare back. Sometimes, early on, there were tears, but eventually only blank stares remained as we were ushered away only to await the next visit from the very nice sad lady, we called Mom. Sometimes it was days, weeks, then months, and then years.

Questions linger inside of me to this very day.

I wanted to honor the memory of Juliet, my mom, even though I contemplated sharing her story. Her story has been the biggest and earliest connection of all my experiences. Through reflection and prayers, I have come to understand why I'm so passionate about helping pregnant women to become less fearful. Why I want to empower them by spreading knowledge and awareness through storytelling.

My mother Juliet became a midwife and then a nurse, a fantastic one by all accounts, at the local teaching hospital in Benin. In Ibadan, she got married in her twenties and had to move about 8 hours from her home and family to be with my father where he worked as a doctor. Shortly after she had me in the 1980s, a short year and eleven months later she had a second daughter. Something was different about that pregnancy. After the first pregnancy, her blood family and in-laws visited. From all the accounts shared, she had a lot of support at that time. She traveled. Apparently, she had a fairly straightforward pregnancy which resulted in a C-section. After the second pregnancy, according to my family, fewer people visited her. There were talks she was very paranoid and stated that people were there to harm or take her babies from her.

In Africa, this behavior was not well understood. Her family and friends thought she made these decisions independently, they did as she asked and stayed away. Sadly, when it was thought to be more and care was attempted by mental health experts, it was refused, as intervention was a taboo in her culture. Rather, alternative medicines were the preferred and safer choice. Unfortunately, that choice wreaked havoc on her marriage. Along with her family, she treated her illness with traditional medicines as would not have been unusual based on the times. Things got better and then a third child was born. Her symptoms worsened—deeper paranoia, and hallucinations. Due to fear and concern for safety, the marriage was dissolved, and custody awarded to my father; it was at this point my mother lost her three children to severe postpartum anxiety and psychosis. Tragically, her early symptoms were thought to be of her own doing, as well as a refusal on her part and her family to seek medical evaluation. Today, early, and persistent support from her *family, medication, and therapy may have resulted in a different outcome for her mental state.*

Losing a life without her children throughout my mom's life was never associated with childbirth. This was because of the culture where she was born. Her mental illness was considered something unfortunate that happened to her. Something that maybe evil spirits had prompted. That perhaps she was choosing to do or that someone had put a curse on her. Every bad outcome was associated with her or a bad decision she made. I wish my mom would have been in a different country or met a professional who saw the decline of her mental health with every birth (paranoia, anxiety, hallucinations). Statistics state that this type of mental decline typically leads to marriage disruption and children removed from the home for their safety, and sometimes, out of extreme fear of the unknown. How many women have lost their fairytale families, weddings, and children to an immense hormonal balance that occurs from pregnancy? As I connect the dots and feel sadness, she didn't have anyone at the time to connect the dots for her and insist she get the help she needed. Instead, her worst fears came through which was the loss of her family, children, and a lifetime of declining mental health till her recent death.

I have a long list of 'if only's' when I think of my mother. Now I understand the warning signs. She had lost her mom at a young age. She moved away from family and married young. She didn't have her network of friends around her. She birthed three children in under four years. She held all the risk factors for a perinatal mood disorder when not factoring in any unknown genetic factors, or history of mental disturbances in her own traumatic childhood.

The mental health decline from her postpartum years, especially since untreated, no readily available therapy resources, or access in her area at the time would have only worsened with the loss of her kids in a custody to her ex-spouse.

My mother Juliet's story can happen to any woman. I hope you can take stock of your life or that of a friend or sister and help them realize their risk factors and plan accordingly by changing those conditions that are within your control. Even consider setting up therapy in

*advance before your due date if you have a history of mental distress.
Setting up support to ensure you get enough sleep from family, friends,
church, neighbors, and have accountability discussions with your
partner to prepare in the event you act out of the ordinary, instead of
confusing or treating mental illness as taboo but being prepared and
have a plan based on any outcomes that arise.*

TAKE BACK YOUR POWER

Taking back our power as mothers means never saying, "That
can't happen to me!"

It means pushing past fear and talking openly about issues
that can affect you.

During the first three months of my twins being born I was
so afraid to think yet alone share with my husband, yet I wasn't
aware that I very well could have been on a similar path as my
mom without realizing it. I was blessed to have support from my
husband, and family and friends. However, I still had a moment
when, because of extreme lack of sleep, I went days only
sleeping 15 minutes. I was so fearful about my babies, who had
severe reflux choking in their sleep. So scared I would wake up
frequently to find them doing so in their sleep. So, I slept with
my nose next to their crib. Their cribs pushed up against my bed
so I could hear any gasping that occurred. The hyper-vigilance
kept my babies alive but caused my mental state to decline.

I started feeling sad and having thoughts that my husband
and mother-in-law would harm my babies and worse take them
away from me. This played over and over in my thoughts, and
even in my dreams, and as a result I couldn't be away even in
another room for any period.

A perinatal mood disorder can look so different for others.
Depression. Uncontrollable crying. Anxiety. Hearing voices. All
symptoms are treatable. Tell your provider or anyone you feel
safe telling. Ask for evaluation by a professional and demand
therapy and medication when needed. If your friend or neighbor

is being distant, or acting differently, remember you may need to intervene. A friend once told me she knew she was in trouble when she felt like she could just sit and stare at a wall all day despite her baby screaming. Thankfully, her husband and mother stepped in. Support is key and sleep as even medications and therapy may take time to kick in. Supervision may be needed and even brief hospitalization, again all treatable even if scary, but the statistics are real especially if previous history of mental illness, or previous pregnancy with perinatal mood disorder, or substance abuses, or very low support, single moms, and/or low socioeconomic status.

Know your own story so you can be prepared.

Save It Forward

For Mama

For the mama currently on her pregnancy journey, I hope you feel empowered and know your rights to safe, accessible, and high levels of maternal health care. Most of all, I hope you understand the incredible feat your body goes through when producing a child, so that you can pay attention to the signs that your body may be trying to tell you. I hope you now have information and skills you can use to advocate for yourself should you ever have to, and how to have very necessary and important conversations with your maternal health team.

For all of us as a collective of amazing and strong women, I hope you have more tools of how you can support that birthing person in your life and in your community. In the rest of this chapter, I want to give even more specifics of the role we all can play and for the future maternal health care we can all put our heads together to design and create for ourselves.

The solutions cannot be left to just our government and healthcare system, it includes us, in fact it must involve us so that the systems we design make sure that all of our voices are at the table and reflected in the solutions. The solution looks like fellow mamas who have been through motherhood supporting one another and lifting each other up not focusing on our differences on how we choose to raise or care for our babies. The solution also involves those waiting patiently to be mama's as they navigate those challenges joining in and supporting those already on their motherhood journey, especially those that are not yet mamas or have decided they don't want to be a mama, know that you are seen loved and heard and you especially can and must play a role in joining the beautiful village it takes to help and support the mama's in your life and community to successfully and safely raise future productive citizens of this nation and world. This lovely village of beautiful diverse women of different backgrounds—experiences and ideals our children can look up to, learn from, and receive the support they need to create a better environment for future generations.

It takes all of us!

FOR EVERYONE

Get to know the pregnant mamas in your circle (work, church, school, and home). Check in on how they are doing, and how you can support. Upgrade your support from just sending and dropping things to FaceTime when you can, especially for my low support mamas, mama with no mothers, single moms, moms that live far from family, those with estranged families.

We are in a new norm of being in a post-pandemic world and these times bring a lot of anxiety for new mothers. As you support mothers, be sensitive to their desire to protect their babies from getting sick. Regardless of how you feel about the pandemic, babies are vulnerable and have weaker immune systems. Please wear your mask and protective gear when helping to support around baby. Wash your hands frequently and be mindful of your own symptoms and exposures regardless of your vaccination status.

Outside of the pandemic, it is good to have your flu shot, and tetanus, diphtheria and pertussis shot, abbreviated TDAP shot if it has been over 5-10 years. These help as well to ensure you protect yourself and baby from these illnesses. Please, when you can, refrain from having a new mama meet you somewhere. It is quite the task to get a newborn out the door, so bring the fun to mama. Offer to pick her up or create opportunities for face-to-face contact. If far away, bridging with FaceTime can be helpful, but know it may be hard to coordinate but if that is mamas only source for support be persistent and do what you can, even by thinking ahead and sending stands or a device to help her multitask as she FaceTimes with you. Help her realize it doesn't need to be perfect for this to happen—she can breastfeed, fold laundry, or wash bottles and cook as she receives that necessary contact.

For the Baby Shower Organizers, the Inner Circle of Trust, and Family Members

I hope this guide has helped you see that throwing a pretty three-hour event is not your only task. You have a role to ensure that mama thrives during and most of all after her pregnancy and there are minor tasks you can help plan and set in motion to ensure this.

If you are helping plan a baby shower, don't simply focus on baby items. Think broader. Consider the level of support that mama has. Would a doula be helpful? Can funds be raised for this instead of say baby books and toys? Can those funds go to a doula instead? It may not be pretty, but remember it is lifesaving. Can you help mama establish a monthly postpartum support calendar? What about sign-up slots for laundry time, scheduled mama walks, and giving mama a 30-minute nap? Or having people volunteer to help mama tidy up for an hour? Be prepared for most moms to say no. It is harder to say no when given options of this or that as opposed to a generic, "Do you need help?" Remember the help and support you give can be the difference between life or death. Mama's brain will tell her she must survive, and she can do it herself, but at what cost? We don't want her back in the hospital. We need both mama and baby to thrive not just survive the first year!

Accountability! Ask mama if she has her 24/7 hospital support squad set up. Offer to join it. She should only have to call and reach one person and the others can activate each other, so you can do a group call and listen in. Do this only if mama is okay with you hearing her medical info, and only if she needs the support. Also, please help create her support plan after baby arrives.

Please do not tell mama to do self-care! That means nothing during postpartum. Remember the hormone changes and sleep deprivation. If mama has multiples with very little support, this can make basic self-care hard on her. She may need time to brush her teeth and shower. So, making the leap to doing more than that feels like climbing a mountain. You may need to book that appointment and take mama to get her hair and nails done. She will feel like a million bucks, and you will make it easier for her to repeat next time.

When offering mama options, consider making them multiple choice. For example, giving mama the option to stay inside and take a long hot bath while you watch her baby for a few hours, or she can spend a few hours getting a main/pedi. Let her know that any choice she makes is fine.

You may need to make follow-up appointments if mama is low support or has shared, she is having a postpartum mental health issue such as depression or anxiety. Follow-up appointments with doctors or therapists can sometimes have long waiting lists, so this is another place where you can offer support. Bring lunch to her home, then sit at the dining room table and don't leave till that appointment is booked, next level support is to offer to take her there and you can listen to your favorite podcast while you wait for mama to finish her appointment.

If you are a far away friend or family with financial means, and if you are helping a low support mom, please get her a postpartum doula. Also consider a night nurse. If mama is part of a church community, you can work with others collect funds for a doula or night nurse. They can be life savers.

For long distance mom, help her plug into community. If cost is a factor, call churches or new mom groups that provide support groups for new mothers. Do the research yourself, as most mothers get overwhelmed and won't go through with it.

Give mama space to share what is really going on. If you ask, "How are you?" She will probably say, "I'm ok." Dig deeper. You can say, "And what else? What is going well? What is not going so well? Is there anything you want to get off your chest?"

Current mamas, this is where you can support your fellow mamas. You can give unbelievable confidence to a new mom by providing space to share her concerns. This type of support was lifesaving for me—it was the type I craved the most. I was grateful when I received the support from friends who were moms already. Please do not judge here. It is tempting for some moms to judge or compete. You are saving a life here. This is postpartum. The stakes are high, so listen—just because it is not being done your way, let her share her feelings. Validate them by saying, "You are not alone." Most moms just want to be heard.

For single moms who are low support, or any mom, really, don't underestimate the power of a hug. An embrace scientifically releases hormones that can lift her mood. Hugs are free! Tell her she is doing amazing. She may not be hearing that at all. Tell her you are proud of where she is. The first four to six months postpartum may lead to depression, anxiety, and even psychosis. Support squad, if you are reading this guide, the biggest fear of any mother is that she will not be seen as a wonderful mother because she is sad or not bonding with baby or having weird thoughts. If a mom shares thoughts that seem disturbing to you up to the first year, lend an ear and listen. Let her get it out. Give her a hug. Don't let her be by herself. Calmly get help from her caregivers and family. Mom's biggest fear is her kids being taken away from her. Stay in touch, please. Make sure she receives the support she needs. Also, understand that some cultures don't believe in mood disorders or postpartum depression. Some see it as taboo, and there are OB-GYNs who are not well educated about mood disorders. Be aware that mama may need to visit a different provider for care.

FOR FUTURE GRANDMOTHERS

If you are the mother to a new mom and you are reading this, and maybe your relationship is strained or not the best, I want you to know your support ranks higher than a partner for reducing stress of a new mother. If you can work on yourself, put your issues aside, and realize you are literally a life saver— just be there for your daughter like you would have wanted when you had her. Her life and safety depend on this. Get therapy and work on your own triggers so that you can be the dream support team for your daughter. It is your daughter's birthright.

FOR EMPLOYERS AND CO-WORKERS

Are you an employer or colleague of pregnant mamas? Can you look at how you can support them? How about discussing the mother's roles and duties when they return to the job in order to give space and ease stress. Don't assume the new mom will function in the same way as prior to baby. Entertain a more flexible schedule and work location when possible. Their lives have changed drastically. Never assume that a mother will be less productive, or unable to perform their job, given the right support, work conditions and flexibilities you will be amazed what a mother is capable of doing intuitively and creatively as these areas of the brain are enhanced during and after pregnancy. The support you give a mother especially during those first five years of child raising comes back to your tens of hundreds fold because of her amazing capacity.

In America, our paid time off is abysmal and may not be changeable. Support creates less stress for returning to work and can go a long way. If you had an employee who just had a big heart surgery, you would ensure that person didn't have to take on the same level of work as their internal healing will take months. Well, the physical and mental healing for a new mother takes months as well — not unlike the patient who underwent major surgery. Try to give new moms the same level of empathy and allowance in the duties and work environment they come back to. Remember, that could be your own mother or daughter being treated that way, so let's all set the standard we would want for our families.

For Maternal Health Care Providers & The Health Care Community

To my colleagues, especially women and mothers in the healthcare field, if you are a mom and or not yet a mom, I want you to look deep inside and understand that your upbringing and experiences may determine how you see and treat others. Never assume you know or can tell how someone feels or that you've experienced their level of pain. Let them tell you. Trust that they know their body best. Your role as policy or protocol gatekeeper must never overcome your oath to do no harm.

Let's make mandatory maternal health resuscitation courses a reality. Why? Every year, my colleagues and I have to take an ACLS and CPR course to maintain our certification. You never know when you might need to thump on someone's chest, but the fact is it can happen any time. The same goes for pregnancy.

I can't tell you the number of times that I walk by someone who is near the end of their pregnancy and say, "Please don't 'pop' now, I don't want to deliver a baby." Then I think, well, do any of us really know what to do if we were stuck in, let's say, a power outage. What could we do in the event help is on the way? Why don't we have maternal courses designed like CPR that we all can take and re-certify in varying levels of difficulty based on the role you play? We take for granted that every woman has access to a hospital or will make in time or that all she has to do is push and the baby will come out and all we need are towels and hot water. What about the placenta? What if help never comes? Do we know what to do with the placenta? We need to demand basic standardized education similar to CPR to increase our awareness of maternal and baby care. We must be able to support our loved ones, especially when help may not be on the way.

Let us put our heads together and design courses that walk us through how to do this. Even though it is rare we will need to help someone give birth, we need to accept that most of us are never that far away from a person who might give birth. And with our understaffed and overflowing hospitals turning people away, it is even more important that we educate ourselves.

Our health care providers are now more specialized than ever, with a dwindling amount that are generalists. We need to certify annually and be able to support the pregnant woman who may not get other services and may need our help. We have a long way to go to build up this curriculum.

Let us remodel our birthing classes, first by re-training and ensuring we standardize the message that is being taught, making sure that these courses not only focus on getting birthing persons through labor but developing robust and affordable curriculums that teach basic self-assessment skills, risk assessment, when and how to escalate concerns in a multitude of settings. Accreditation and auditing to make sure that the content of the information shared in these classes are up to date.

Such courses will help rural providers who don't have access to or see these life-threatening events to stay up to date in the standard treatments. Again, so we don't pointlessly lose another mama to a preventable pregnancy ailment.

FOR TECHNOLOGY ENTHUSIASTS

Every day in my career, business, and day-to-day life, I'm amazed at some of the technological tools we now have at the tip of our fingers to help make some things that took us so long to do before taking a fraction of the time. Whether it was the detachable CD player I used to have in my car just 15 years ago with an album of CDs, I would thumb through in my car to decide which song I wanted to hear. Fast forward to today. Today I simply pay Apple Music a monthly subscription and I can play music in my car by Bluetooth. I can keep my kids entertained with any song or video they choose. I no longer need boxes of CDs or DVDs in my car anymore.

Then I think about how little has changed in some clinics that provide maternal health.

I remember my first time learning how to check a blood pressure in medical school, using the manual cuff, and using my stethoscope to listen for the pulse, and yes admitting to myself did I really hear it at that point and re-doing it. Skip to today. Today a stethoscope is hardly needed. Now, you slap it around your wrist or arm and a machine tells you the blood pressure. However, there are still many clinics using the manual cuff, even though pregnancy blood pressure readings must be accurate.

Why don't we ensure the most up-to-date technology that reduces error in our vital signs are being used? Why is health care so slow to update its technology? Why is technology so slow to be used to update health care workflows? I think about myself during my postpartum period with pre-eclampsia. What it would have been like to wear my Apple watch to record my heart rate, breathing and blood pressure? How about having that sync up to my medical record chart that is being observed and monitored by a nurse in my maternal health provider's office? After all, it is that person's job to monitor those in vulnerable times like 6 weeks postpartum or more if high risk. Both Mama and the health teams can be taught to observe trends and receive alerts of deviations from the norm as well as empower patients to report the same. In a future world before the patient even realizes what's going, she would receive a call from the health care staff to come in for an evaluation to make sure things are okay.

I dream of such a world where technology is used to anticipate the health care needs of our patients, especially during their most vulnerable times. I hope we cannot only think and invest in using technology to improve our lives outside of our health, but also re-prioritize and invest in using technology to support an overworked healthcare workforce. More so to protect our vulnerable populations who every day endure the effects that arise from these inefficiencies in our health care system. Encouraging our young girls to learn and join fields of technology, engineering, and computers is important—who better to connect the dots to create lifesaving technology for women than other women. My heart smiled when I heard of organizations such as Girls Who Code, which teaches young girls to code and create computer programs and more. Organizations like these must be supported and encouraged.

Ask yourself if you or someone you know works in the technology space—especially in innovation. Do applications exist that can be of great use in improving the care of our mothers and future mothers?

For Our Children

No matter how you were raised, give your children a voice. Do not prescribe to old models that children's opinions don't matter, or they are to be seen and not heard. Be mindful of how that has carried itself in your life. Let us only pass things that uplift our children to thrive in this world.

Start early. As soon as your child can speak. Give them the words to describe what they are feeling. Teach them how to communicate that something hurts or feels strange. Before their doctor's visit, prepare them. Perform little skits with them and describe the healthcare environment, the role of the nurse, the staff, the doctor, and the pharmacist. Don't teach them the doctor is all powerful or place the doctor on a platform or pedestal. Teach them they will work together with a team of dedicated individuals all doing their best to care for them. Teach them that guess what they are part of that team, because they can tell us what feels right, or wrong, if something is better or worse. They can tell you their parent anytime judgement free when something feels different. Please teach them that not only our physical bodies can get sick but also our mind, our brain. Teach them that just because no one else can see it, that doesn't mean it's not real. Teach them they can always bring you their problems and concerns. Together you can ask for help to figure it out.

Teach your kids that the brain has chemicals, and sometimes it can cause a person to get sad, nervous, or scared. On occasion, someone may need the help of a doctor, medicine, or a therapist to get better. Prepare your kids for life so that when they become adults they don't have to struggle and resist asking for help when they need it most. As humans, it is inevitable our bodies and mind will break, either slowly over time or suddenly.

Describe to them early how the brain and mind and body can get sick. You don't have to wait and hope they will one day learn it in their future biology class one day.

Prepare your girls early for their menstrual period. Don't be afraid to be honest. Tell them how it can be different, you can say things like "some people have pain, nausea, they feel sad and angry during their monthly period, some people have heavy bleeding and others…"

Get a menstrual kit ready well in advance so that it is there for them. Instilling this communication early will teach your child valuable skills later to help them be able to stand up for themselves and communicate confidently and in a timely way with their healthcare teams in their futures.

A CALL TO ACTION

We must act for the future of every person who wants to be a birthing person someday, and for those who already are.

Demand the standards we want for our maternal health care system.

What type of care do we want for our children and their children? We must be specific and help to be a part of the solution. We know the problems and we are excellent at pointing them out. But we must collectively form a think tank to decide what are minor changes we can perform today to reach a state of zero for **preventable** maternal complications and mortality in our society and world.

Share this guide. Support, and potentially save a friend, sister, neighbor, coworker, and yes, even stranger.

A woman not being heard for whatever the reason, and especially for her skin color, based on the bias of the provider, or health care staff, is not a freaking option! Take the pearls in this guide and do the most important thing you can do to change your outcomes: self-empowerment through knowledge of the big picture and awareness. Join the think tank!

I never want another woman feeling paralyzed like I did.

Or worse—meet their end due to lack of basic tools and information.

We must choose to not tolerate any more preventable deaths and join in the growing community that is working hard to lead this effort. The power of our stories around these issues are grossly misunderstood and I hope as you read this you too can share and grow and potentially save someone and I pray you or your loved ones never know what it feels like to be unseen and unheard or worse be a statistic of maternal mortality.

The world needs you!

The Journey Ahead

Congratulations for reaching the end of this guide. Thank you for letting me lead you during this journey. I would have loved to have been there for those who are gone. I am grateful to be a small part of the journey to support a mama in your life more intentionally and informed or on your journey to one day being a mother.

You should notice some profound changes after going through the content in this guide and doing the journal prompts, for visualizing and affirming worth and value of women and mothers in society.

As a more informed person you now have a better foundation to support yourself and others starting early in understanding the numbers and what they mean so that fear and inaction do not prevail. Also becoming more comfortable knowing your own body and health and why no one else can dictate to you about how you feel, or what gets done to you without your input and consent.

I hope I have inspired you to start early with your children to learn how to notice how they feel and practice talking with their health care provider confidently. It is never too early. Many of our adult struggles may be tied to lack of awareness or exposure during our childhood. Let your children be more prepared to view health care staff as their guides - available to help them to feel better.

I am confident you now have built a more solid foundation for preparing for babies' arrival but also equally for mama's journey as well as how to better celebrate in a more holistic way that allows mama to thrive and not just survive motherhood. One that ensures mom is supported, cared for, and knows who she can rely on when and if things go wrong.

The theme of support runs strongly in this guide, and I want to emphasize it as the antidote to most of the issues we face in our society. I hope it inspires you to plan better not just for birth but to ensure a strong support system is in place, whether from your family, community or paid for in doulas, coaches. To this day I regret not hiring a doula. I'm grateful for doulas. They play a powerful role in the life of a mama. Supported mamas have opportunities to rest more, strengthen their mental health, become more resilient, and adapt to stress. They also have the chance to recover faster, and reduce their risk for chronic illness and pregnancy complications. Try to work creatively to support mamas who may not want help or support because of their postpartum mental health—they may actually need it more.

Continue the conversations be sure to share your story as you never know who it will help or inspire. Use some of the continued reading resources to continue to inform yourself, listen to podcasts, read articles, and join local community groups for continued support and awareness on all that we can look forward to as we improve maternal health in our country together side by side.

Read the next section to review resources I have discovered along the journey writing this guide. Follow along for future additional content, updates, and other wellness topics to achieve a balanced well life at www.saveyourselfmama.com.

Resources

The **Elizabeth Hold Reyna Scholarship Endowment** was established in 2013 to provide 1-2 students annually with a scholarship to the University of Houston Hilton College of Global Hospitality and Management. If you would like to donate to honor the memory of our dear Liz, you can do so here: https://giving.uh.edu/gift/?allocation=HC18178HA1044

Listen

The following podcasts provide information and resources for moms-to-be and postpartum mothers.

- The Birth Hour: This podcast provides invaluable advice to expecting mothers and new parents, focusing on birth stories, postpartum health, and parenting tips. It's hosted by an experienced midwife, nurse, and doula, so you can always expect reliable information.

- Down to birth: This podcast shares powerful birth stories and is hosted by individuals with experiences in midwifery, advocacy, childbirth education, postpartum support and breast feeding.
- Black Mamas Matter: This podcast is dedicated to supporting and uplifting Black moms. It covers topics such as pregnancy, postpartum, parenting, and maternal health.
- Black Mom Village: This podcast is about celebrating Black motherhood and empowering Black moms. It covers topics such as parenting, health and wellness, and financial literacy.
- The Brown Mama Monologues: This podcast is all about creating space to discuss the unique experiences of Black motherhood. It covers topics such as body image, mental health, and parenting in the Black community.
- Mamas Talk: This podcast focuses on the unique experiences of Black mothers. It covers topics such as self-care, relationships, and parenting.

RESEARCH

The following resources offer information on where to give birth and research to help you find the best and safest place for care and delivery.

- US News & World Report: Ranks hospitals based on a variety of criteria, including patient experience and safety.
- Medicare.gov: Provides ratings and reviews of hospitals based on patient experience, safety, and quality of care.

- Consumer Reports: Provides ratings and reviews of hospitals based on patient feedback, safety, and quality of care.
- The Joint Commission: An independent organization that evaluates hospitals to ensure they meet quality and safety standards.
- Baby-Friendly USA: An organization that evaluates hospitals based on their ability to provide safe and supportive environments for breastfeeding mothers.

FOLLOW

These organizations are doing amazing work. Follow them to find out continued efforts.

- Every Mother Counts: Every Mother Counts is a global organization committed to making pregnancy and childbirth safe for every mother, everywhere.
- March of Dimes: The March of Dimes is a national organization that works to improve the health of mothers and babies.
- The White Ribbon Alliance: The White Ribbon Alliance is a global network of organizations and individuals committed to ending preventable maternal deaths.
- Safe Motherhood Initiative: The Safe Motherhood Initiative is a global network of organizations and individuals dedicated to preventing maternal mortality and morbidity.
- Mothers Matter: Mothers Matter is a global campaign to raise awareness of maternal health and reduce maternal mortality.
- The Maternal Health Task Force: The Maternal Health Task Force is an international organization that works

to improve the quality and accessibility of maternal health care.

- Maternal Health Now: Maternal Health Now is a global organization that works to reduce maternal mortality and morbidity through advocacy, education, and policy development.
- Girlswhocode: I have been excited about this group because the girls who are girls who code will one day be moms who code and the creativity, they will bring will no doubt help some of our lacking in structure and technology that affects mothers today
- Mom First. (Formerly Marshall Plan for Moms): Fighting to get moms support they deserve like childcare, paid leave, and equal pay.

INFORMATION ON WHERE TO GIVE BIRTH AND CLASSIFICATION

Birthcenters.org - American association of birth centers standards for birth centers: https://www.acog.org/clinical/clinical-guidance/obstetric-care-consensus/articles/2019/08/levels-of-maternal-care

POSTPARTUM AND MENTAL HEALTH

Remember to support mama after birth, and care for her mental health as well. The following resources help with both:

- Postpartum Support International: https://www.postpartum.net/
- American Psychological Association: https://www.apa.org/pi/about/publications/caregivers/resources
- American College of Nurse-Midwives: https://www.midwife.org/postpartum-care

- Centers for Disease Control and Prevention: https://www.cdc.gov/reproductivehealth/maternalinfanthealth/postpartum-care.html
- U.S. Department of Health & Human Services: https://www.womenshealth.gov/mental-health/postpartum-depression

The following websites provide information on warning signs for pre-eclampsia and maternal stroke:

- Mayo Clinic - https://www.mayoclinic.org/diseases-conditions/preeclampsia/symptoms-causes/syc-20372782
- American Pregnancy Association - https://americanpregnancy.org/pregnancy-complications/preeclampsia/
- National Institute of Health - https://www.nichd.nih.gov/health/topics/preeclampsia
- World Health Organization - https://www.who.int/news-room/fact-sheets/detail/maternal-stroke

Statistics and Data

- Centers for Disease Control and Prevention (CDC): https://www.cdc.gov/reproductivehealth/maternal-mortality/disparities-pregnancy-related-deaths/infographic.html.
- World Health Organization: https://www.who.int/reproductivehealth/topics/maternal_health/maternal-mortality/en/

HEAR HER CAMPAIGN

- Black Mamas Matter Alliance: The Black Mamas Matter Alliance is a national organization dedicated to advancing maternal health equity and reproductive justice for Black mothers.
- National Birth Equity Collaborative: The National Birth Equity Collaborative is a national organization that works to eliminate racial and ethnic disparities in birth outcomes.
- Sisters in Loss: Sisters in Loss is a national organization that provides support and resources to families who have experienced the death of a baby or mother during pregnancy or childbirth.
- Black Mamas Wellness Collective: The Black Mamas Wellness Collective is an organization that works to reduce maternal mortality and morbidity in the Black community through education, advocacy, and policy reform.
- SisterSong: SisterSong is a national organization that works to improve the reproductive health and rights of women of color.

Acknowledgments

I dedicate this book to all the incredible women and mothers gone too soon on or after their journey to motherhood. I include those I had the special privilege of knowing and being raised by, however briefly, and those I never knew but are no longer here because of complications during pregnancy. For those lost from not being heard or seen, know your death will not be in vain. Your story will live on and help us all to do better for our mamas.

To my grandma Maria: You truly are "The Teacher". Thank you for showing me what a fierce, independent woman and entrepreneur looked like. You illustrated how to make a legacy for yourself and your family while creating solutions for the world. For you, it was access to quality schooling for all despite your background or socioeconomic status and the value of helping others. Because of you, countless children in Africa gained access to top-notch education you built from only one room to a series of Montessori, primary, secondary schools, and colleges.

To my mother Juliet: I can never know your full history because I lost you twice—in mind and now in body. However, your spirit and legacy live on as a cause. I hope to always remain a part of the solution—helping women like you, who with every birth surrendered pieces of their mental health and eventually a lifetime of memories of children and grandchildren. Your story helped me, and it will help many others support a community of new mothers. I pray your story inspires us all to strive for a future of abundant and accessible mental health care during pregnancy. In all corners of the world, let us aspire to preventable death and ensure the loss of quality of life is a thing of the past.

To Liz: I will always cherish your friendship and sisterhood. Our relationship continues to comfort me daily. Your kindness, hospitality, and story continue to help those you left behind. I am so glad you received your one wish you shared with me — to be a mother. We all think of you every day for teaching us to make life happen, not waiting for it to happen and I truly see the "Liz" moments and trails you give us. I just know your story will inspire and help so many women and mothers.

Memories of Liz from a few of her friends:

"Liz loved love and was already in love by fifth grade. She had a different earring for each day in the month of December leading up to Christmas. She supported any business idea I had and would help me test out recipes. She was my biggest supporter; she was my most favorite person to look forward to during Christmas. It was us against the world!" ~Allison

"Everyone Liz met fell in love with her. It was my favorite thing about her. She made us all laugh no matter what. On a trip to New Orleans, she gave nicknames to our friends. She called herself Princess beignet and our friend Irene, Mama Muffuletta. In school, she always faced her challenges head on and never gave up. We studied so many nights. One final we had to study for coincided with our friend Anne's going away party so we went to the party which was at a club took our flashcards and would dance to a song then go study flashcards before going back to the dance floor." ~Kanwal

"Liz loved her family ferociously and was very protective. I remember her telling me she was pregnant. She was so overjoyed about being a mom. She said, "I'm quitting my job, I'm getting a soccer van and I want to just be the best mama to my babies." It felt like she knew exactly what she wanted in life and made it happen! Period! Wear her cap and gown on graduation day (no clothes under). Check! Get married to the man of her dreams. Check! Move to Boston after college. Check! Become a business travel sales manager. Check! Live in Houston and start raising her family. CHECK!" ~Kanwal

"It's impossible to single out a memory of Liz. She was great friends with so many. I had a book in high school of Liz quotes and saved silly names and words she made up…we laughed so hard. She was so adventurous and exposed me to so much. Dancing. Travel. She would pick me up in the 'big red bus', her Buick, and we would just drive around together doing her errands, and laughing so hard. It was our favorite thing to do together." ~Sandhya

"So many belly laughs. My fav was my first-time fishing during a visit to her parent's ranch and I thought I caught a huge fish, but it was a branch. We laughed so hard. laughter that comes from deep in your belly that your sides hurt were my most fun memories with Liz in college that wouldn't have happened without Liz." ~Anna

"My best moments in college were hanging with Liz and going dancing. We didn't go to clubs for boys, we went just to dance our butts off. She named a dance move after me called *The Anne*. She was so funny, sweet, and considerate." ~Anne

To Yulin: The tragic passing of you and your dear husband Jon in that car accident was the first horrific senseless death I ever experienced. You taught me that just because we grew up without a powerful voice because of our upbringing and cultures, that it is never too late to hold your ground and do what you feel is right for yourself. You encouraged me to take a stand even when it is not popular—indeed when we have to distance ourselves from those who don't see us or allow our light to shine. Thank you for your early friendship, when I never felt deserving of—and needed it most.

To my OB-GYN and the amazing NICU staff that took great care of our babies during their one-month NICU stay: Thank you for making sure I felt seen and heard.

To my editor, Keisha Gilchrist-Broomes: I'm still having goosebumps and know it was divine that I found you as you made the possibility of this becoming a book so much more real and possible. Thanks for your amazing work helping me hone my voice, my message, and my stories.

To the cover illustrator, Jeric S. Tan: thank you capturing the essence of motherhood in the cover.

I am incredibly grateful for Priya, Abigail, Kim, Marina, Pamela, and Kamran's unwavering support in my maternal journey. From recognizing my potential, encouraging me to use my voice, coaching and educating me, to going above and beyond to provide support and allow me the rest I needed, their leadership served as an inspiration and will never be forgotten. I'm truly blessed to have had such incredible mentors and colleagues who understand that being a working mother is a balancing act and make sure I get the support I need.

To my clinical team: Thank you for allowing me to lead you even when I wasn't sure what that meant. The skills I have accrued leading you are what have helped me thrive and not just survive. I learn from each of you daily.

To Laura, Emily Sutherland, and the rest of the Gayle Well Foundation for early onset Alzheimer's board members: You showed me what advocacy looks like, and how to put the heart or should I say humanity back in creating policy and doing the work. Emily, the masterclass about telling your story encouraged me to dust off the cobwebs and just keep writing and going. I won't forget your generosity.

To Dr. Hold, Eva Hold, Louis, and family, for allowing me to share the story of dear sweet Liz and baby Evan who left us far too soon. You are always going to be a part of my family.

To my dad: Thank you for understanding and supporting me during the journey of writing this guide and giving your expertise as an OB-GYN who practiced in rural Nigeria. I know life has not always been easy, and it forced you to make tough decisions that as a parent I don't envy, but I appreciate you always ensuring my education and safety where a priority and showing me the ethics of hard work and doing the right thing both in medicine and in life.

To my surrogate mothers Lati, Patricia, my late Grandma Maria, my mother-in-law Jane, and Lucy, for helping always to fill the immense gap in the lives of me and my siblings left by not having our mother present, I now know how hard and selfless it is to make space for another person's child. My surrogate mothers, my sisters and all my friends, for at some point or other without realizing it you played the compulsory role of mother that I have craved and always will, most of all for inspiring me, and giving me glimpses into what a good mother is based on how you raised your kids. I look up to each of you in different ways. You have all provided tremendous support to me that has been more appreciated than you will know. Collectively, you have all been my mom squad.

To my siblings, cousins, and family: Thank you for always believing in me and being there to support me.

To my girl squad and friends, Hannah, Irene, Kanwal, Julissa, Crystal, Lan, Heather, Sandhya, Prishal, Anne, Anna, Xiao, Joni, Eve, Kara, Catherine, Liz S., Liz B. , Melodye, Sarah, Jen, Steph, Laura, Valerie, Jessica, Miracle, Katie, Mariah, Mia, my co-workers, and anyone I may have left out: Thank you for the calls, advice, walks, foods, gifts, hand-me-downs, gifts, and listening to my dreams. You also helped me in ways I can't quantify to thrive through my first years as a mother. Whether you knew you were part of my life giving support squad or not, I'm grateful for your generosity.

To my husband, David, for enduring the endless chats about the book while juggling twin toddlers and always offering sound advice, as well as the encouragement to never give up on any of my dreams, thank you for loving me no matter what. I love you.

To my twin daughters, Aria, and Olivia, for the blessing of being your mother. My biggest prayer is you get to grow up to know the love of your mother. Thank you for pushing me to be more creative and authentic, so I can be a good role model for both of you. I still recall the long hours waiting to see you in the NICU that led me to start journaling, and now has led me to write this book. You both inspire me to grow daily. I love you both more than words can ever describe.

About the Author

Ivy Cocuzzi, PA-C wears many roles with gratitude. She is a wife, mother to twin toddlers, and oncologic vascular access and ultrasound proceduralist physician associate—an educator and healthcare front line leader with over 15 years of experience. Additionally, as a life coach and student of public health and social work, she enjoys helping people realize their potential especially in the areas of wellness, relationships, and creativity. Ivy strives to encourage others to impact the world and gain access to knowledge through her life stories, education, and experience. She loves to grow her faith and spirituality and build and learn with her community through her courses and podcast (Sweet Sorrella Stories). Ivy loves to travel, improve her French, play peek-a-boo with her daughters, enjoy coffee dates and strolls with her husband, and walk her 13-year-old Golden Retriever/Aussie Shepherd mix, Paix.

You can visit Ivy online and find additional resources at http://www.sweetsorrella.com/and connect with her through Instagram and Facebook @sweetsorrella. Get free digital resources on www.saveyourselfmama.com like pdfs and workbooks to help tell your medical story.